AF225978

REREADING GENESIS 1–11
WITH A LOOK INTO
REVELATION 18:1—22:7

REREADING GENESIS 1–11
WITH A LOOK INTO
REVELATION 18:1—22:7

A POST-CHRISTENDOM PERSPECTIVE

James Strickler

RESOURCE *Publications* • Eugene, Oregon

REREADING GENESIS 1–11 WITH A LOOK INTO REVELATION 18:1—22:7
A Post-Christendom Perspective

Resource Publications
An Imprint of Wipf and Stock Publishers
199 W. 8th Ave., Suite 3
Eugene, OR 97401

www.wipfandstock.com

PAPERBACK ISBN: 978-1-6667-3866-7
HARDCOVER ISBN: 978-1-6667-9966-8
EBOOK ISBN: 978-1-6667-9967-5

VERSION NUMBER 021023

CONTENTS

INTRODUCTION

Why study Gen 1–11? The best reason I know is provided by Terrence Fretheim who makes the following argument (see his *God and World in the Old Testament*). One doesn't begin a novel, or to tell a story, in chapter 3. Nor does one begin a novel in chapter 2. One begins in chapter 1. The reason is though the elements and principles developed in chapter 1 may not directly appear throughout the rest of the book, they nonetheless perform a primary informative function over the events in the rest of the book. So if one skips (or badly misunderstands) the first chapter, one will badly misunderstand the events recorded in the rest of the book. Fretheim surmises that beginning to read and understand the Older Testament at Exodus is like our chapter 3 (he is an OT theologian, but the argument should also be applied to cover the Newer Testament as well. For the first chapter for the Newer Testament isn't Mt. 1, but Gen 1 since Gen 1 is the first chapter in scriptural canon). Nor does one begin to read and understand the Older Testament in Gen 12 (which he likens to our chapter 2). One begins to read and understand the Older Testament in chapter 1 (which he, and other OT theologians, liken to Gen 1–11).

I do not devalue creation by assuming what unfortunately has become the understanding of scriptural canon as simply representing Salvation History. As Fretheim says, "God's redemptive work does not occur in a vacuum: Gods work in creation provides the basis for God's work in redemption: God's work in redemption fulfils God's work in creation" (*God and World in the Old*

Testament, 112). Salvation history's understanding of history devalues Gen 1–11 as simply a prologue to the rest of the scriptural canon. I understand Gen 1–11 as having the primary informative capacity over the rest of the scriptural canon that follows.

Up front I must share the suggestion that influences these essays. This suggestion led me to the hypothesis that Gen 1–11 must be informed by the Creator God *Elohim* in Gen 1, and further led me to read Gen 1–11 through the eyes of *Elohim* rather than through the eyes of the YHWH taught by Christendom Christianity. I have come to realize that that *YHWH* from Gen 2 on needs to be, and must be, informed by the creation God *Elohim* of the first narrative, and that is my thesis.

As I began this study I thought that I was fairly familiar with the stories of Gen 1–11. I found out that I'd never really heard what the stories say, even from the usual Christendom orthodox perspective (the perspective that I was raised in). That perspective seems to understand that the *YHWH* tradition of the second creation narrative in Ge. 2 had, and has, ultimate informing capacity over the *Elohist* tradition of the first narrative in Gen 1.

My first readings of the stories in Gen 1–11 was from the Christendom's *Yahwist* perspective that I was raised in. I found that the readings told vastly different stories in many ways than what I thought I knew. Then, as a result of reading from that perspective and further study, I thought about *Elohim* in Gen 1. Further informative experience came from seeing a book titled *The Second Story of Creation: A Prologue to History* and I thought, "Oh yeah, what about Gen 1?"

Yes Gen 2, in its written form, is historically older than Gen 1; but what tradition was Gen 2 speaking from and into? Raine Eiser. in *The Chalice and the Blade,* looks into the cultures of Old Europe (Europe before the Steppe invasions from Russia) which were long before Gen 2 was developed. One might question what does the cultures of Old Europe have to do with the ancient Near East? A fair and good question. Perhaps they can be somewhat informative of our understanding of the life of the people of the ancient Near East before they developed into the higher cultures of Egypt and

Mesopotamia. At least there seems to be some remembering of a life that resembles what I suggest images *Elohim*. These cultures seemed to have a much more egalitarian life between the sexes and were largely agrarian. We see such ways developed in our look into the creative God of Gen 1 (Elohim) that we understand should inform our understanding of *YHWH* in Gen 2ff.

Who knows how long it took the *Elohist* tradition to develop?). In my understanding neither Gen 1, 2, or any part of Gen 1–11 can be simply dismissed and slighted as only being a simple "prologue." What does Gen 1 tell us about the creation God *Elohim* of the first narrative? I knew that the *Elohim* authors of Gen 1 were younger than the *YHWH* authors of Gen 2, and even though the authors of Gen 1 are understood to be priests of the *YHWH* cult they still began their editing of Genesis with the *Elohist* narrative. So given that the authors were priests of the *YHWH* cult it is interesting that they thought that there was some importance behind the *YHWH* tradition that is to be informed by the *Elohim* tradition in Gen 1 rather than to start the editing of Genesis (an editing which has come down to us) with the *YHWH* tradition in Gen 2. In other words, why didn't they start Gen 1:1 "In the beginning when *YHWH* . . ."? Rather, they started Gen 1:1 "In the beginning when *Elohim* . . ." Who is *Elohim*? This provided me a reason to explore the person of *Elohim* in Gen 1. And the *YHWH* cult continues to realize (at least in the editing) some importance in the *Elohim* tradition. Who am I (or anyone else) to belittle whatever that importance was/is, or to slight Gen 1–11 as simply being a simple prologue? I suggest that at least some of that importance has to do with the characteristics of *Elohim* developed in the first narrative, and is to inform one's understanding of who *YHWH* is in Gen 2ff. Does *YHWH* echo these characteristics of *Elohim* or not? My suggestion is that *YHWH* is to echo *Elohim*, and when *YHWH* does not echo *Elohim* then one must question who that *YHWH* is. Does *YHWH* echo *Elohim*, or is *YHWH* the God of the nationalistic cult of Israel (who is dominative over the other, is patriarchal, and is both hierocratic and anthropocentric) that does not (for the most part) echo *Elohim*?

This resulted in my further reading of Gen 1–11 through the eyes of *Elohim* rather than simply through the eyes of Yahweh.

One also thinks of the common critique that the God of the NT does not look like the God of the OT. My response to that critique is yes and no (my common response to most critiques and questions). Yes, the God of the NT looks like *Elohim* of Gen 1 (and the *YHWH* who echoes *Elohim*); and no, the God of the NT does not look like a *YHWH* who does not echo *Elohim* (I understand that much of the prophetic tradition in the OT questions the *YWHW* tradition in the same way).

My final reading of Gen 1–11 is from the perspective of *Elohim* developed in the first narrative and has provided other new understandings of who this creation God is (not only who *Elohim* is, and who *YHWH* is to echo; so also who *YHWH* is). Many of these new understandings offer some radically new insights (at least for me) and are developed in reading the stories of Gen 1–11 through the eyes of *Elohim*. How these new insights are to inform one's understanding of the development of *YHWH* in the development of the following cultic traditions are also effected. I intend to share with you some of these understandings in the following essays at least some of these new insights that I see.

I further wondered about the conversations in Job 38–39 where God describes the God-self in terms of creation. One would think that would take me back to the creation God in Gen 1, but before that took me to Gen 1 it took me to the opening chapters of Job. In Job 2:7 the RSV says, "So [s]atan (the adversary) went out from the presence of the Lord. . . ." In verse 10 Job begins to respond to his wife's comment in v. 9b, "Curse God, and die," with the response in 10b, "Shall we receive the good at the hand of God. . . ." In these three verses we go from *YHWH* (the Lord) in v. 7 to *Elohim* (God) in vv. 9–10 (I take many of my Hebrew questions to K. C. Hanson and he affirmed the translations I assumed).

Was Job just responding to his wife who first uses *Elohim* for God in 9b? However, K. C. said Job's response in 10b was more emphatic than his wife's simple use of *Elohim* in 9b. In 10b it is *ha Elohim* (the God). The God; not a God, not *YHWH*, not even

YHWH Elohim But the God of creation, *Elohim*; and the conversations in Job 38–39 echo that. Now we can go back to Gen 1 and find out about the creation God *Elohim*.

That pretty much cements the issue for me. I say "pretty much" because I realize that issue is much more convoluted than to simply say that the above arguments have entirely resolved the issue for me. But close enough to begin talk in terms of it being cemented.

So lets find out something else about *Elohim* in Gen 1.

Claus Westermann earlier observed that theology has become too anthropologically centered (which I understand to be the typical Christendom Theology developed by Augustine, and his followers). And though the so-called "reformers" (Luther, Calvin, and Zwingli, among others) brought a newness to the theology developed under Augustine, this "reformation" is still too influenced by Augustine and his followers (see David Wright's essay "Augustine and the Transformation of Baptism" in Kreider, ed., *The Origins of Christendom in the West*, 287–310. This essay looks at how Augustine transformed baptism from baptism understood in the early church to Christendom's understanding of baptism. Also see the last chapter in Kreider's *The Patient Ferment of the Early Church*, which looks at how Augustine transformed the early church's understanding of patience. Also see George Tinker's discussion concerning how Augustine established a priority of time and temporal sequence over spatiality or place in *Spirit and Resistance*, 93–95). One should also mention Julian of Eclanum. He carried on an ongoing debate with Augustine for twenty years concerning Augustine's thought about sin, death, and sexual desire. Augustine's hierarchical view says that sin causes death and is linked with, and caused by, sexual desire. Julian's argument was that physical death was caused by nature (is part of life's experience in nature), and that sexual desire was nature's way that eventually leads to reproduction which was nature's way of not simply being controlled by death. After Augustine's death, and some further debate over the issue by the church, the church accepted Augustine's thought and branded Julian and his thought as heretical.

Westermann laments that in general theology has moved away too quickly from the creational theology developed in Gen 1–11 by saying, "In other words, once theology has imperceptibly become detached from Creator-Creation, the necessary consequence is that it must gradually become an anthropology and begin to degenerate from within and collapse around us. . . . And so the question must be put: what sort of God is he [*sic*] who does everything for the salvation of man [*sic*] but clearly has nothing to do with real history?" (*Creation*, 3–4, which includes the rest of creation. Also see Tinker, *Spirit and Resistance*, 111–115). I must also note another book that has definitely informed my thoughts for the following essays: it is Alan Kreider's *The Patient Ferment of the Early Church* on the early church's historical background (also see his *The Change of Conversion and the Origin of Christendom*). This may seem odd when studying Gen 1–11, but I see that the creational theology developed in Gen 1–11 is significantly echoed in Jesus (on the universal aspects of Jesus and Gen 1–11, see Westermann, *Creation*, 111–23). It is Jesus who says, "I and the Father [*sic*] [*Elohim*] are one" (John 14:9–11). Jesus echoes *Elohim* (not the other way around. I must note my indebtedness to Fretheim in the theological insights in the following essays).

I've been encouraged to say something about my conversion in the late fall of 1971 (for it definitely informs my interpretation of Scripture and ever since I've been on a quest to find out who this God I was converted into is). I wasn't converted into Christendom Christianity even though I was raised in it. Some three to four years before my conversion I came to the conclusion that churchianity (what I called Christendom Christianity) as an option for my life was one step below suicide. It eventually came to that, but against the odds I woke up (and some people will say in a number of ways). What I referred to then as churchianity I came to later understand was politically established by Constantine and was given its most influential theological development by Augustine (see John Sanders, "How Do We Decide What God Is Like?" in Gaiser and Throntveit, eds., *"And God Saw That It Was Good: Essays On Creation and God In Honor of Terence E. Fretheim*, 154–62. Above I've shared some of my wonderings about Augustine). If I wasn't converted into chur-chianity/Christendom Christianity (which still, as an option for my life, is one step below suicide), then what was I converted into?

I was converted into what I have since come to refer to as Post-Christendom Christianity. Not simply the societal/historical reality known as Post-Christendom, but I suggest here the beginning of a theologically biblical alternative to Christendom Christianity that I call Post-Christendom Christianity (which, in my estimation, looks more like Early Christianity than Christendom Christianity does, though the early church also became too influenced by the dominant cultural surroundings. Even before Constantine). My reading Gen 1–11 through *Elohim*'s eyes also addressed some of the wonderings I had about who this God was that I was converted into (see my conclusions).

I also disagree with Christendom's understanding of church history. We agree on at least one thing, and that is that there was only one reformation in church history. We, however, will disagree when that reformation took place, and under who. It seems to me that the reformation is best placed at 314 AD under Constantine because before that date church was done one way, and after that date church is done another way. Is that not a reformation? However, I don't think Constantine thought up all the pathologies, idolatries, and ideologies of this reformation (that can be seen to begin to develop, at least, around 250 AD; and has only been further developed by Augustine and Christendom. Perhaps that should be taken back to the events recorded in 1 Sam 8 when Israel wanted a king, where it should also be noted that God not only accepted a king, but only after Samuel explained what a king would do to them, and later in 1 Sam 12:12–25 also went on to acknowledge the place and importance of kings/governments. But, of course; that is derived from the events recorded in Gen 3:1–7 and must be taken back to Gen 1). Though a king wasn't *Elohim*'s choice of how Israel was to be governed. However, *Elohim* does learn from prior experience (note *Elohim*'s work at changing the "not good" to good in Gen 2; as well as the learning of the necessary, and rightful, place of kings and governments in 1 Sam 12:12–25).

What happened under Luther, Calvin, Zwingli, et al. is essentially the same orthodoxy developed by Catholic Christendom of the time; just dressed up a little differently. But it is essentially still the same Constantinian/Augustinian Orthodoxy of the Catholic Church of the time. The only continuing counterreformation to the Christendom's Orthodoxy, and the only counter-reformation to Constantine's reformation in 314 AD, came under the sixteenth century Anabaptists (though they were typically on the run, or in prison, and so were unable to develop their theology much).

Another aspect of myself that informs my understanding is my interest in, and interaction with, Native American cultures (in both reservation and urban settings. For a good description on the importance of oral traditions, and the different perceptions of oral traditions, see Abram, *Becoming Animal*, 267–78). I am certainly not *sola scriptura*. However, both poles of understanding Scripture (both the fundamentalist pole and the contextualist pole, defined below) approach scriptural understanding by beginning at the same place (that Scripture represents divine inspiration). And though the truth of Scripture rarely reaches the extremes of either pole, the truth doesn't simply dismiss the poles either. The truth, however, usually wanders through (and constantly moves between) both poles.

Something else I should let the reader know about me is that I'm way more Johannine than Synoptic. That is not to say that I dismiss the Synoptic tradition, but that is to say that the Synoptic tradition does not occupy a primary place in my thinking. I understand that the Johannine tradition brings several necessary critiques to the Synoptic tradition, and several corrections as well. When one compares Matthew's opening with the opening of John's Gospel one notices a difference. Matthew begins with Abraham. Though I know what Matthew is doing and why, the scriptural canon does not begin in Gen 11:27 when Abraham (actually Abram) is first mentioned. And scriptural canon certainly does not begin in Gen 12. That is just the beginning of patriarchal history. The "just" in the sentence above isn't to dismiss or belittle patriarchal history at all but is to acknowledge that the scriptural canon doesn't begin in Gen 12 (on patriarchal history see Paul Borgman, *Genesis: The Story We Haven't Heard*). Scriptural canon starts in the beginning at Gen 1:1, and John's Gospel also starts there as well (also see Lois Malcolm, "The Crucified Messiah and Divine Suffering in the Old Testament," in Gaiser and Throntviet, *"And God Saw That It Was Good,"* 136–44).

It must also be noted that though Gen 1–11 is often referred to as chapter 1 of the scriptural canon, and since Gen 1 is the first chapter of Gen 1–11, it therefore has the same informing capacity over Gen 1–11 as Gen 1–11 has over the rest of the scriptural canon that is developed after it.

In Gen 1 we will find that the creator God *Elohim* is in intimate relationship with all creation (*Elohim* is relational). What effects this web of created relationships effects *Elohim* as Fretheim says in *Creation Untamed* (131–135; see also his *God and the World in the Old Testament: A Relational Theology of Creation*). That effect is noticed right from the start of the creation process in Gen 1:2–4. In the first story of creation we also find *Elohim* sharing the creative power with that which has already been created (in Gen 1:2–4a the light, which is valued in 1:4b; and that the separated light is good for its purpose). And this also establishes a kenosis theme (self-emptying) that Paul sees Jesus echoing in Phil 2:5–11. The *kenosis* theme here is that *Elohim* does not simply decide alone on how creation will develop. The creation's input is encouraged (and necessary) which also implies a self-limitation because the self-emptying means that one has applied a limitation upon that which is emptied. And this is a divine self-limitation, and that right from the start! The kenosis theme here is that *Elohim* chooses not to simply dictate creation without the input of that which has already been created (in Gen 1:2–4 the light which enlivens the already present earth). We will follow this kenosis theme through the eleven chapters as it gets developed in the chapters and occurs several times in almost all of the eleven chapters.

If one doesn't understand that the theology of Gen 1–11 describes the character of *Elohim* then one must wonder what is happening? We will see in Gen 1–11 the development of *Elohim* who is the Creator of love, who shares the creative power with creation, is in intimate relationship with all creation, and is *Elohim* who owns kenosis (a self-emptying God of self-limitation). If one isn't informed by this knowledge then one badly skews or outright misunderstands the character of *Elohim* and YHWH developed in the rest of the scriptural canon that follows (one is simply left with a retributive theology rather than a theology of love. See Kenton Starks, *"Fake News" Theology*). Starks does a good job discussing the foundational approach to understanding Scripture (a fundamentalist and literalist approach to understanding of Scripture), and the contextual approach to understanding Scripture (open to being informed by outside sources); and that the proper way to understand either approach is that they must be informed by the Creator of love. *Elohim* is the Creator of love and is best developed in Gen 1 (and 1–11) and is further incarnated in Jesus (and is incarnated in the way of Jesus, or as Kreider argues patience (see his *Patient Ferment of the Early Church*).

My study of Gen 1–11 comes after my long intensive study of John's Apocalypse (some twenty-eight years and counting, but for the last seven years my intensive study has been on Gen 1–11, and yet my Revelation study remains open). The last several years of my intensive Revelation study was devoted to looking at the usual translations of Revelation by Christendom (particularly the English translations) and comparing them to the Greek text of Revelation. I found out that the usual translations of Christendom often don't translate the Greek text well (sometimes just wrong, but more usually providing such an anemic translation that it doesn't allow for certain images developed in the Greek text to inform our English translation). I ended my Revelation study with the realization that Christendom got the translation wrong (and therefore our understanding of the text). So, given that they got the ending bookend to scriptural canon wrong, what about the opening bookend (Gen 1–11)? Though I didn't begin this study with the assumption that Christendom does get the translation and understanding of the opening bookend wrong, I nonetheless was open to wondering. What does the text say, and what do other scholars say about it?

Indeed, I didn't have to go far in my study (just to the first verse of Gen 1) to find out that they do badly misunderstand what's going on in Gen 1–11, and as I proceeded through the eleven chapters I came to find that my study was given a certain PhD quality. Not that I pursued the study as a PhD thesis (nor do I think it is—I certainly didn't write the original essays as such, though they have since been developed into more of a defense for the outlandish conclusions I seemed to come to than just the simpler writing of the original essays). The PhD quality I'm thinking of is that the study **P**iled on **h**igher and **D**eeper the evidence that Christendom does in fact misunderstand the opening bookend.

It may seem that I come down hard on Christendom Christianity (and perhaps I do), but Christendom Christianity can't simply be dismissed in its entirety either. However, perhaps the most subversive thing about Christendom Christianity is that some of it does indeed look like the way of Jesus (who echoes *Elohim*). But, in my estimation, much of it does not. In saying that I don't mean to excuse myself from the destruction Christendom Christianity has caused (for I too am an heir of that way and fully am culpable as a result). I do, however, call for growth and change from our being too influenced by Augustinian thought and Constantinian politics, and to move forward in new theological ways that are rooted in the characteristics I see in *Elohim* (as I understand they are to inform our understanding of YHWH), and return to the hegemony of God (See Tinker, *Spirit and Resistance*, 98–99).

In the following essays I only discuss the aspects of the text that seem to me need to be discussed to enlighten what is going on in the text, but before you read the following essays or any other commentary on Gen 1–11; read Gen 1–11 first. Try to read it fresh, in such a way as that you've never heard the chapters before, read them, or know anything about them. Read the chapters as for the first time and let them tell you what they say. Don't read them in such a way as to try to tell them what you think they're supposed to say. Only after such work should you read the following essays and then other commentaries. Some commentaries proceed in such a way as to tell the stories what we think they're supposed to say (usually under the guidance of Augustine and his followers), but there are many good commentaries that can add to the discussion on aspects of the text that I don't cover. Some of the essays are quite short and those other commentaries can, and should, be consulted to fill out one's understanding of the text. A couple of essays that I will highlight is "Gen 1:1—2:4a" for that is where we are first introduced to Elohim and "The First Covenant, Gen 9:8–17; and its Fulfillment, Rev 18:1–22:7." It contains what I understand is the absolute bare minimal teaching on Revelation (particularly its ending). Though one should read the prior essays leading up to it first as they inform one's understanding of it. In it I also compare and liken Jesus with *Elohim* arguing against Paul who simply compares and likens Jesus to Adam (cf. 2 Cor. 5:21; Rom 5:12–17). Though I so not dismiss or deny this argument I see it as simplistic and understand that Jesus is more preemtively linked with *Elohim* rather than simply with Adam.

It must be noted that part of the Older Testament's experience of *Elohim* (as well as the Newer Testament) is that *Elohim* is experienced as the one of *hesed* (steadfast love, mercy, Ps 107:1; cf. Mic 6:8), and that this *hesed* of *Elohim* triumphs over judgment (Jas 2:13). I offer the following insight from someone that is praised by, at least, part of Christendom:

> This is the courtesy of Deep Heaven; that when you mean well, He [God] always takes you to have meant better than you knew. (C. S. Lewis, *That Hideous Strength*, 226–227)

And to borrow one of Chesterton's thoughts for my defense:

> (The next best thing to really being inside of Christendom is to be really outside of it. (G. K Chesterton, "The Everlasting Man" in *Collected Works of G. K. Chesterton*, 2:143)

Does my subjectivity noted above enable me to see the images of *Elohim* developed in Gen 1–11 that others miss? Perhaps, given my influences mentioned above (this paragraph is influenced by Alan Kreider's *The Patient Ferment of the Early Church*, 4). I am certainly influenced (in both good, and badly limited ways) how I understand the opening chapters of Genesis. But then I ask myself why has it taken me so long to see this development that addresses so many of the wonderings about God that I've had since my conversion? What other things do I not see, or misread? That correction must be left to others.

In Rom 12:2 Paul encourages us not to be conformed to this world (its dominating order) but to be transformed by the renewal of your mind (I also see that this passage connects rights with greed which is an anthropocentric arrogance. It's wrong to emphasize one's rights over one's responsibilities for that does not image the kenosis of *Elohim*). I've argued for this renewal that I see is first argued in Gen 1 and is further theologically developed through chapter 11. It is the difference between the dominating civilization and the partnering way of relational sharing (see Eisler, *The Chalice and the Blade*). And Paul refers to this renewal as the will of God (Elohim).

After writing this study I had time to look into Norman C. Habel's Earth Bible Project. After reading the following study one will see that I share much in common with the Project.

CHAPTER I

THE FIRST CREATION STORY
Gen 1:1—2:4a

It must be noticed that Gen 1:1 is notoriously difficult to translate, and biblical Hebrew itself presents its own difficulties when it comes to talking about only one authoritative or accurate meaning of a particular text as expressed by Jacqueline Osherow (an English professor and poet, she is also Jewish and a Hebrew scholar). She says, "I love . . . the unrestricted multiplicity and infinite plasticity of the poetic line—above all, its refusal to limit itself to a single puny statement, but rather its insistence on saying at least two opposite things at once . . ." ("That We May Live and Not Die," in Kissileff, ed., *Reading Genesis*, 221–36). She continues by noting a similarity with the Biblical Hebrew language (in its having no punctuation or vowels), and Gen 1 is an epic liturgical, poetic, prose-narrative; it is essentially a priestly report. Although the best translations of the Hebrew in the first verse, "In the beginning God created the heavens and the earth," is perhaps correct, it must be noted that this creator God here is *Elohim* and that it refers to the heavens in the plural. I understand this to introduce *Elohim* who is to inform all that follows; and to include all the heavens (including the highest heaven that I understand is the celestial realm, the *Elohim*'s home that we now have no direct access to). My use of Creator is not meant to simply think of the Creator solely in male terms (for *Elohim* is a feminine noun with a masculine plural ending. It's also interesting that *Shekhinah*, "God's presence," in Hebrew is a feminine noun) and is my personal bias (hence my being personally comfortable use of "Creator," but I prefer *Elohim*). It must also be noted that the largest part of the heavens is what we know as sky (a realm that contains this earth's atmosphere where the birds fly, but also creation's realm of the sun, moon, and the movable stars—the planets—or our solar system, and the third heaven [a realm of outer space], which is both of this creation in that it can be explored and measured to some degree, but also has its never-ending quality which echoes the eternal quality of *Elohim*). The third heaven (which Paul refers to in 2 Cor 12:2), rather than simply being some celestial place, overlaps this creation with the highest heaven (mystery one). If the highest heaven didn't overlap this creation it would set up a dualism that denies the inherent relationship between the heavens (of which I note only four as four is the universal number) and the earth. Rather than a dualism between the heavens and the earth a dance is a more appropriate symbol. The heavens and earth work together and are parts of one whole. However, "In the beginning *Elohim* created the heavens and the earth" is perhaps most likely correct as far as the Hebrew goes and treats the poetry well. I, however, prefer John Walton's preference of, "When God (*Elohim*) began to create the heavens and the earth" (*The Lost World of Genesis One*, and see the *Tanakh*. Gen 1:1. But these essays are more informed by Terence E. Fretheim's *God and the World in the Old Testament*, and his *Creation Untamed* is just as good, shorter, and a somewhat easier read. Also see Chan and Strawn, eds., *What Kind of God?*). Walton's suggestion also makes better sense of the following verses in the first chapter and doesn't simply play loose with the Hebrew for it is a possible translation of the Hebrew; and it does make the best sense of following two verses. Fretheim observes that the Hebrew verb for create (*bara'*) refers to both original creation and continuing creation (*God and the World*, 7–9, 37), and only refers to divine creation (having no object of material or means, and that the Creator is the subject of the verb. No material means does carry an appropriate analogy to the *Elohim*'s act of creation, Fretheim, *Pentateuch*, 73). Verse 1 is a summary of chapter 1 as well as an introduction to it. I agree with George Tinker that creation must be the starting point of any theology (Tinker, *American Indian Liberation*, 37–38).

Verse 2 talks of the *Elohim*'s *ruach* (wind, tempest, gale, or breath; and is feminine) and *Elohim* is a feminine noun for deity with a masculine ending leaving no room for patriarchy of any kind). In Latin *ruach* is rightly translated as spiritus. But that translation is too easily spiritualized. Fretheim observes that the spiritual and the physical/material realms are not simply separate realms. They overlap each other (another mystery, Fretheim, *The Suffering of God*, 102, and see Abram, *The Spell of the Sensuous*, 3–29). The *ruach* seems to be the air in the wind (or life energy force) and is not simply nothing or "empty space." Air lies between all things and is even within us (to live we inhale and exhale continuously energizing us). This *ruach* hovers over the darkness of the void (*bohu*, void, but not nothingness. *Bohu* also carries the meaning of being filled with the building blocks of matter—Schroder, *The Science of God*, 57) of the deep, which is upon the earth (which isn't the earth that we know cause it was a void, not nothingness; but still was). The void provides the *ruach* something to hover over (this void does not seem to be a void of materiality for the earth already is before *Elohim begins to create*, another mystery). Rather this materiality of darkness seems to be void of organization, productivity, purpose, and good function; and the earth is, but is unproductive and uninhabitable. Yet the earth already is before the *ruach* hovers over it. This does not set up a dual aspect of the divinity. Where the void or the earth came from is not a question the primitive world addressed (some sort of materiality was assumed to be before *Elohim* began to create, another mystery). I prefer "breath" rather than "wind," "tempest," or "Spirit" to translate *ruach* because it addresses the intimate presence and life of the *Elohim*, and *Elohim*'s presence with all creation that the rest of the chapter establishes; and because v. 3 has the *Elohim* speaking into this deep void (Ps 29 talks a lot about *YHWH*'s voice, *Elohim*'s breath, and vv. 3a and 10a particularly say, "The voice of *YHWH* is upon, and enthroned, over the waters." The darkness of the void was also known as waters. *YHWH* is enthroned over this flood, a mystery noted above). Gen 1:1 seems to note that *Elohim* was before the mass of disordered materiality (another mystery) which was simply assumed to be the deep, or waters. Also, though v. 1 speaks of *Elohim* creating (*bara'*, which is not linked to the material), verse 4 goes on to speak in terms of the *Elohim* separating the light from the darkness (*badal*, which assumes some sort of material, which is then separated). This darkness already seems to contain a physical material (perhaps the light was mixed in with the darkness, but then *Elohim* didn't create whatever was in the void but created the nonmaterial light). William Brown observes that this light also represents *Elohim*'s radiance (see "Joy and the Art of Cosmic Maintenance," in Gaiser and Throntveit, *"And God Saw That It Was Good,"* 28). Susan Brind Morrow suggests the probability that everything is made of light (*Wolves and Honey*, 68–69; and follow her discussion concerning weather and air. If this is true, that all things were made from light, which I think is true and is therefore a precursor to [and within all of creation that follows] then this establishes *Elohim*'s relationship with all parts of creation equally and does not allow for any hierarchism of any kind. Each part of creation is endowed with the same worth before *Elohim*). *Elohim* created light, which was valued as good and was further separated out from the darkness (we are also to separate light from darkness, cf. Matt 6:22–23; 7:1–27). This light that *Elohim* separated from the dark was to give the material order good purpose, function, and productivity. Was this material from the act of separation of the light from a material in the darkness or was it from the light itself (this remains as one of the mysteries)? This order, purpose, function, and productivity had never been seen before (neither had the light).

The remaining darkness now becomes known as "chaos" (that which is not good). I put quotation marks around "chaos" for chaos isn't mentioned in v. 2, and because in v. 2 this void or deep (or this mass of materiality) is neutral—neither good nor bad—just dark (without order, purpose, productivity, or good function). Perhaps this void in v. 2 (which sometime later in v. 4 after the light is separated from the darkness is when the chaos is established) has more to do with reciprocity than simple opposition? It must be pointed out that any duality (be it between good and evil, spirit and matter, or the choice between the good road or the bad road) only comes to light with the existence of its opposite but is still somehow related to its opposite (however, the choice between the two is still ours). Perhaps we should not simply refer to the way of the bad road simply as evil, perhaps there is more of a reciprocity here than not (for in v. 2 the dark of the void is neutral, and just is. This is also perhaps a nod to some of the other creation myths of the eastern Mediterranean, for Israel's creation myth echoes them in significant ways. In some other eastern Mediterranean creation myths the earth just was, before the gods began to create). It must be noted that this void/deep and earth already had its presence before *Elohim* spoke into it light and began separating the light from the darkness of the void (which was not simply nothingness for it was already there). It also provides *Elohim* with something that *Elohim's ruach* hovers over, and to speak into (hence "When *Elohim* began to create . . .").

Though v. 2 speaks of *Elohim's ruach* hovering over, or moving upon, the void or deep Ellen Davis notes another picture of what is happening in vv.2–3, and the rest of the narrative. It comes from the great primeval and mythological poem about Wisdom in Prov 8:22–31. The poem notes Wisdom's playfulness with creation, creation's playfulness with *Elohim*, and especially creation's playfulness with the created humans (Davis, *Proverbs, Ecclesiastes, and the Song of Songs*, 66–69. It should also be noted the playfulness that the trickster, usually the coyote, plays in indigenous American thought—a teacher. We know him best as Wile E. Coyote.)

And according to the best science of the day (pre-history's, and early Judaism's up to the exile; not today's science, or later Judaism's) this material mass was just assumed to be. Verse 3 somewhat defines that mass of materiality by what the *Elohim* calls forth and values and leaves behind (on evaluation see Fretheim, *God and the World*, 40–42). *Elohim* calls forth light and values it as good (*towb*). Fretheim argues that this just doesn't describe an objective good but should rather be understood as describing something that is good to achieve its purpose (Fretheim, *God and the World*, 52–53. Also see Lefebvre, *The Liturgy Of Creation*, 181–82, and see Westermann *Creation*, 60–61, 63–64).

Now what is this light in v. 3? I suggest that this light is somewhat the same as the light that is created in v. 14, and somewhat different. It's not simply light as we usually know it (the sun, moon, stars, or what comes from a light bulb). That doesn't get created until day 4 (vv. 14–19), and yet is somewhat the same for it (like all creation) is developed from this light in v. 3 (another mystery). What is *Elohim*'s light in day 1? I agree with the suggestion that we learn that this mass of materiality that is left in v. 4 is a disordered chaos. Though there is some sort of materiality in this void (there is already the earth that seems to be covered with deep waters). This darkness is thought of as something disordered and different from our usual concept of material (another mystery). It is both disordered and purposeless (and as a result having no productivity or good function). *Elohim* gives at least part of this mass of materiality (the light which is separated from the darkness) its goodness; its order, productivity, purpose, and good function (thus allowing for a continual creating as what is created is good to achieve its purpose; a continuing creation which is its good function, another mystery). I also understand that this separation is the beginning of time. But it must be observed that place and spatiality was before time (the earth of v. 1 is before the first day of v. 4. Time begins and moves within the space of the earth, see Tinker, *Spirit and Resistance*), and therefore should have more influence over the narrative, and us, than the concept of time (see George E. Tinker, *Spirit and Resistance*, 26, 46).·

This light is separated from the darkness, and *Elohim* values it as good. What does this value mean? To leave the translation simply as "and it was good" is not wrong, but it can also be translated (and makes better sense of the phrase in rest of the chapter) as "it is good for its purpose" (Fretheim, *God and the World*, 52–53).

The phrase does not simply mean to speak of an objective good as opposed to some sort of an objective bad (though it also probably has that in view). I suggest, however, that it makes better sense of the phrase (and the rest of the chapter) to understand the phrase to mean, "it is good for its purpose." Its purpose (the achievement of which is its good function) is to transcend itself (or develop) into a more fully complete creation. *Elohim* doesn't simply create out of nothing, but always creates from that which has already been created, or (as in verse 3) speaking light into the darkness of v. 2 (does Elohim speak the light into the darkness or was it already in the darkness just not light? For the light wasn't in verse 2 but is spoken into the already darkness by *Elohim* in v. 3). It must be further explained that *Elohim* doesn't share the creative power in v. 2. However, in v. 3 *Elohim* values the light, which was then separated from the darkness. Then the remaining darkness is not good (the rest of the mass of materiality) and this pictures *Elohim* sharing the creative power with the then-separated light (for it is valued as good). The darkness is therefore not good, and is now considered to be chaos, which still has no order (and is therefore unproductive and having no good purpose or good function that *Elohim* values). *Elohim* does, however, share the creative power with that which *Elohim* values (the valued and separated light) as being good for its purpose (that being the ability to develop *Elohim*'s creation into a better and more full creation. Is it this value of good that invests the material into the light? Another mystery).

This raises at least a couple of questions. The first being, "Did *Elohim* create out of nothing or not?" The second being, "What is *Elohim*'s relationship with creation, and what are its implications?" This understanding of the opening verses of Genesis allows for both a *yes* and *no* answer to the first question. No, *Elohim* didn't necessarily create the original material out of nothing (the darkness was already and *bara'* is never linked up with the material. Which leaves the question did the material come from the dark void or from the good value of the light?). And yes, *Elohim* created out of nothing because the light *Elohim* brought in v. 3, and its valuation in v. 4 had never been seen before. But there perhaps was no material in the original light in v. 3 (for *bara'* is never linked up with material). However, there seems to be material in v. 4 for this light is valued as good for its purpose to continually create. So where did the material in the light come from? Was it in the valuing of light as good, or from the act of separation from the darkness (or was material somehow also in the light? Mysteries). But in spite of any confusion the day's work is ended, there was morning and there was evening day one (again noting time's beginning after the spatiality of the earth in v. 1).

But what of *Elohim*'s relation with creation, and what are its implications? To speak of *Elohim*'s breath hovering over the void/deep in v. 2 and to picture *Elohim* speaking into the void/deep in v. 3 denotes an intensely personal and intimate relationship with the darkness (and its added light) with the following creation; and that right from the beginning of the creative act! One's breath is an intimate part of oneself, and when one speaks. To speak one exhales allowing one to speak, which also informs that other personality. And this breath (*ruach*) hovered over the void/deep (one must also note that humans can exhale or speak only after one inhales; see Abram, *The Spell of the Senuous*, 225–60. Though we cannot speak without first inhaling that is not to infer that *Elohim* must first inhale in order to speak. *Elohim* speaks out of *Elohim*'s being (*Elohim*'s light, or radiance *Elohim*'s life). This addresses *Elohim*'s intimate presence with creation rather than it addresses some need for *Elohim* to inhale, another mystery). This intimate and personal relationship that starts in day 1 is also developed through the rest of the days of chapter 1 (on the universal relationship of *Elohim* with all of creation see Fretheim, *Jeremiah*, 167–76). Here we see *Elohim* sharing the creative power with the separated light of day 1. This is the first act of kenosis (self-emptying) that we see in Gen 1–11, for *Elohim* does not simply dictate the development of creation without expecting, and allowing for, creation's input; but vulnerably allows creation's input (mystery that allows and expects partnership with all creation). We will need to follow this kenotic theme at least through chapter 1, as well as through chapter 11.

Gen 1:6–8 tells us about day 2. Again *Elohim* speaks into the waters (apparently the remaining darkness of the void/deep of v. 2 are waters, some sort of material). The waters are separated by the firmament. We saw *Elohim* creating light in v. 3, and here is developed, or evolves into the firmament that separates the waters (this study calls into question both fundamentalist creation arguments and evolution or scientific arguments. This study sees both arguments as false arguments. See Vine Deloria Jr.'s *Evolution, Creationism, and Other Modern Myths* where he sees both arguments, both creationism and the scientific argument of evolution, as modern myths and offers other thoughts). In v. 7 we are told that the Creator "made" the firmament (mystery). *Elohim* can now make because "to make" involves material things and there is now a material to make with. This is the second self-emptying of *Elohim*, for *Elohim* just doesn't dictatorially control how creation will develop; but allows creation itself to have its input (and each time creation is allowed its input is a kenotic act of *Elohim* and shows a continuing of creation even up to the present). *Elohim* again values this separation as good for its purpose. The day's work is ended, and evening comes.

In day 2 we see *Elohim* sharing the creative power with that which had already been created in day 1 (the light). This doesn't picture an omniscient *Elohim* (one who knows everything so as to dictate the development of the creation as the Hellenistic understanding of omniscience informs us). If *Elohim* shares the creative power with that which had already been created then *Elohim* doesn't simply dictate creation's outcome (or know it), nor simply owns the creative power; but vulnerably leaves some creativity up to that which has already been created and shares the creative power with the good light (which is a counter to the usual Hellenistic understanding of omniscience. This relationship with all creation, this self-emptying partnership before and with all creation is to inform not only humans but all of creation as well. Speaking of Hellenism, I don't think Hellenism has been overly helpful for either Judaism or Christianity [Oscar Cullmann, *Immorality of the Soul or Resurrection of the Dead?*] not to mention creation itself).

In Gen 1:9–13 (day 3) we first see that the heavens are gathered into one place, and the waters under the heavens are separated (and the dry land appears as a result). It was so (not simply by the action of *Elohim*, but also with the help of the firmament created in vv. 6–8 which itself was an act of *Elohim* and the created light). And *Elohim* called (or named) the dry land earth (the firmament isn't simply the earth or the heavens, mystery), while the waters were gathered together into what we know as seas. And *Elolhim* values this development as good for its purpose. And the dry land also, "puts forth vegetation (plants yielding seed, and fruit trees bearing fruit in which is their seed, each according to its kind, upon the earth)." *Elohim* again values this development as good for its purpose. This evaluation is doubled in v. 12. Michael LeFebvre rightly observes that this doubling emphasizes the fruitfulness of the first three days of establishing order (*The Liturgy Of Creation*). The day's work is ended, and night comes once more.

In Gen 1:14–19 (day 4) *Elohim* creates light (this light is somewhat the same and somewhat different than the light created in v. 3 as noted above). This light is what we experience as light and is also a result of that first light that was created (as well as the firmament created in day 2, and the development of day 3; but always moved into action by *Elohim*). *Elohim* places the lights in the heavens (the sky of this creation, the solar system and space. Both the solar system and the universe can be measured in some form. Therefore they are present in the spatiality of this creation and not some celestial place, or the highest heaven. But the universe also has a neverending quality to it, and therefore can also be referred to as having a celestial quality too). This sky is above the firmament in which the day and the night are separated and serve as signs of the season, days, and years—to order time (and the seven-day structure of the first narrative also serves lectionary and calendrical purposes, Michael LeFebvre, *The Liturgy Of Creation*. However, it must be emphasized that the time of the seven-day structure lies within, or after, the place of the earth in v. 2, and the lights are placed in the place of the heavens. On the equivalence between the first six days of Gen 1 and the fifteen billion years of the universe see *The Science of God* by Schroeder); and so these lights in the sky give light upon the earth, and control time. Again it is so according to *Elohim*'s word (however, not just as a result of *Elohim*'s word, but also because of the previous creations). And so *Elohim* made (*'asah* not *bara'* because *'asah* [made] relates to an action that includes the material) the sun and the moon (each ruling Its time of day and night respectively), and the stars also (marking the turn of the year). The importance of this is to put sun worship in its place as well as astrology (*Elohim* created the sun, moon, and the stars; and put them in their place. Worship *Elohim*!). *Elohim* values this development as good for its purpose. Again the day's work is ended, and night comes again breaking into day 5.

In vv. 20–23 (day 5) we learn that the waters that were gathered into seas producing "swarms of living creatures," and birds are created and given the ability to fly across the firmament of the heavens (note that the heavens/sky are not just above the firmament, but part of the firmament, for though the firmament is not simply the earth or the heavens/sky, it does, however, lie behind the earth and the heavens; as well as within them, mystery. And note that *Elohim* works with the seas and the firmament of the sky to develop the sea creatures but creates [*bara'*] birds who fly in the sky!). There should be some hesitancy in referring to the seas as "mother seas" (I nonetheless question this hesitancy, there is both a yes and no aspect to this and any other metaphor. Yes, the sea creatures come from the seas, or as "mother earth" cause vegetative life, and all living beings, come from the earth. However, *bara'* once again appears with the creation of birds (so the materiality of the earth is not simply included in the creation of birds, as least in the author's mind, and *Elohim* is behind and within all creation). In v. 21 *Elohim* makes the sea creatures from the already-established oceans and creates the birds. *Elohim* again values this development as good for its purpose. And *Elohim* blessed them, saying, "be fruitful and multiply and fill the waters of the seas, and let the birds multiply on the earth." This valuing as "good for its purpose" is the original blessing and is further described here as being fruitful and multiplying (though it must be noted that though fruitfulness expands our understanding of multiplying, fruitfulness does not simply repeat multiplying). Again the day's work is ended, and night comes once more.

In vv. 24–25 (day 6, phase 1) we see *Elohim* creating the living creatures from the already established earth, each according to its kind (I think of these, and the vegetation, as the original earthlings for it is just not just *Elohim's* word that brings them forth, but the earth as well, hence, the original earthlings). This negation makes sense, and also somewhat escapes me. Again *Elohim* values this development as good for its purpose, but there is no talk of the day's work as being ended, just leading into the second phase.

Genesis 1:26–31 (day 6, phase 2) is of importance simply as recognized by the length of the recording of this phase of the day's events (however, it must be noted that the importance must be tempered with the fact that humans share day 6 with the creation of the animals. The English word animal comes from the Latin word *animus* and means endowed with mind or spirit). Animal comes from the Latin *animus* meaning endowed with mind or spirit). *Elohim* invites the help of others, perhaps not just that which has already been created, but also with the help of what the rest of what the OT knows as the council of the gods (probably not entirely different realms, mystery. See Abram's *The Spell of the Sensuous*, 3–29, but the rest of the book is also highly recommended), and perhaps this is also a nod to the polytheism of other culture's creation stories around the eastern Mediterranean that informs Israel's. At least the "us" seems to require that monotheism be informed by henotheism (the adherence to one dominant God while there are also lesser gods, angels, or messengers. In the words of Anne Primavesi, "God *is/is not* man, and God *is/is not* woman, God *is/is not* Nature," *From Apocalypse to Genesis*, 171). This web of relationships established by *Elohim* (on the web of relationships see Abram, *The Spell of the Sensuous*, 31–72) seems to require that henotheism/monotheism (note Melchizedek's *Elohim Elyon* [God

Most High], *Tanakh* Gen 14:18 note c. I'm indebted to Borgman for this insight. See his *Genesis*, 74. This also echoes the syncretism of the earlier goddess worship that was also polytheistic and monotheistic *The Chalice and the Blade*, 21–24). This web of relationships also informs creation in terms of a panentheism (not pantheism, but panentheism; the belief or doctrine that God is greater than the universe and pervades and interpenetrates every part of the universe and also extends beyond space and time. In the words of Anne Primavesi God *is/is not* man, God *is/is not* woman, God *is/is not* Nature (*From Apocalypse to Genesis*, 171, but also see Deloria, *Evolution, Creationism, and Other Modern Myths*, 148). Fretheim further speaks on how this passage informs humans on the vocation given us by *Elohim* (*God and the World*, 262–63). Here Fretheim talks in terms of task along with vocation, and that the vocation/task is for both the human and the nonhuman realms (Fretheim, *God and the World*, 273–84, and see *Creation, Fall, and, and Flood*, 35. On the rightful place of anthropomorphisms in Gen 1 see Lefebvre, *The Liturgy Of Creation*). Fretheim also says that there is no racial separation between humans, and he observes that this passage both universalizes the Yahweh-Israel relationship; and that Gen 9:6 notes that this image suffers no loss because of sin (*Creation, Fall and Flood*, 64). Genesis 1:26 seems to speak more of human theomorphism than of *Elohim's* anthropomorphism (Fretheim, *The Suffering of* God, 104–5; cf. Ps. 8:3–5). In essence it speaks more of the dignity humans have before, and with, *Elohim*. As Westermann says, "The biblical declaration about the dignity of man [*sic*] differs from the secular view in this, that it says something not only about human worth but also about the meaning of human existence; man [*sic*]—everyman [*sic*]—is created for this purpose: namely, that something may happen between him and God and that thereby his life may receive a meaning" (*Creation*, 60).

Then we get to what has been the more problematic passage of the verse, "let them have dominion (on dominion see Fretheim, *Creation Untamed*, 34) over the fish of the sea, and over the birds of the air, and over the cattle, and every creeping thing that creeps upon the earth."

What is this dominion? Does it suggest some sort of oppressive dominative quality over the other (this "other" includes all of the creation) that is commonly understood and realized in the human realm? It does not! The dominion refers to *Elohim*'s royal dominion that is to bring blessings to all under the dominion. And that human "freedom" does not extend to being however and whoever we, as humans, want to be; for humans are created free to be *Elohim*'s image and ambassadors to, and for, creation. Indeed freedom goes beyond just human freedom (to be who *Elohim* created us to be) to also include the rest of the created order (or beings) to be free in order to be who they were created to be (see Fretheim, *Creation Untamed*, 86–88). Instead, as Fretheim observes, "Man [*sic*] is God's viceroy; his responsibility is to maintain and enforce God's claim to dominion. It may be said that man [*sic*] is the intermediary between God and the creation" (*Creation, Fall, and Flood*, 65). We must continue to look further as to how this dominion is described. It is *Elohim*'s dominion (not ours), and it is affirmed that *Elohim* made humans in the *Elohim*'s own image (mystery). *Bara'* does not appear in this verse. The word "made," *'aseph*, entails a certain amount of materiality, portrayed in 2:7, whereas *bara'* is not linked up with the material), emphasizing that humans were made (here *'aseph* is used and corresponds to the dust in 2:7) as both male and female (a relationship). Relationship is part of *Elohim*'s image and is who we as humans are to be. Lefebrve also observes that the Hebrew verbs do not address gender differences but our sociality, "This word choice indicates the expectation of a entire race, not merely of (individual) human beings but of human societies (i.e., "reproducing families organizing royally in God's image," *The Liturgy Of Creation*, 176)." Verse 27 once again has *Elohim* creating humans (again the word *bara'* appears and indicates a creation from something other than a simple materiality, but this creation (in 2:7) is also with the dust of materiality, another mystery). In v. 28 *Elohim* reaffirms the original blessing of v. 22 and goes on to affirm human "subduing" as a part of what dominion constitutes (we now have the beginning of further "descriptions" regarding *Elohim*'s understanding of this dominion. As part of *Elohim*'s good creation humans have something to do, to subdue; mystery). Above I put "descriptions" in quotations because there will be more descriptions concerning *Elohim*'s idea what this dominion is to look like. Here the humans are encouraged to also subdue (this subduing implies that the rest of the earth, that in v. 2 still remained without order, and notes here that we are to bring order to the rest of the disordered earth. I'm not simply comfortable with referring to earth as disordered. However, humans are co-creators with *Elohim* because that creation is not a finished product. There is something for humans to do to help develop creation [Fretheim, *Creation Untamed*, 31–37], not to dominate in some form of a human dominative oppression over the other (this also indicates that the "good" creation was never complete without the further work of humans). To subdue a field is to bring it under cultivation from its wild (disordered) state (and not to harm it in any way), and implies that creation, even with all *Elohim*'s work, is still incomplete. The human must, through the exercise of this vocation/task, help to bring creation to its fullest potential (on the continuing act of creation, not only regarding human creation but also the continuing creation of all created beings from 1:3 on, see Fretheim, *Creation Untamed*, 9–37). *Elohim* further describes the food source for the created animals (I include the humans under animals instead of referring to them simply as earthlings because the term earthling, though it also can refer to humans as noted in 2:7, does not allow for the necessary difference this passage observes between humans and the other earthlings). A further difference is that *Elohim* created (*bara'*) humans but also includes *'aseph* along with *bara'*, but simply made (*'aseph*) the animals (Lefebvre, *The Liturgy Of Creation*, 140–41), and emphasizes that vegetation is to be food for everything that has the breath of life; the *ruach* of *Elohim* (this includes both the animals and humans, cf. 7:4, though Lefebrve makes a good argument that this does not simply refer to all as being vegetarian, *The Liturgy Of Creation*, 179–80). On the sensate possibilities of plants (which might also be related to other inanimate created beings) see Suzanne Simard's *Finding The Mother Tree* (also see Peter Wohlleben, *The Hidden Life of Trees*). The day's work is ended, and night comes once more, but it must be noted that both understand that nature is ruled by relationships that are symbiotically cooperative more than one that is competitive.

The animate world, according to the primitive/pre-historic mind, perceived that all created things are created beings, and is better recognized as persons. Not just animate life, but everything lives; vegetative life, soil, rocks, water, air, wind (which is also the *Elohim*'s breath), sunlight, etc. (see Anne Primavesi, *From Apocalypse to Genesis*, 150–51 where she quotes Martin Buber as noting our need to relate to all things as persons). For all are created through *Elohim*'s *ruach* and so live. The best way into the mind and perception of pre-historic humans that I know of is from a western point of view is David Abram's *The Spell of the Sensuous*, but his insights are deepened with George Tinker's *Spirit and Resistance*. Tinker is a professor at Iliff School of Theology. He is also a member of the Osage Nation (to further dialogue between Native Americans and Christianity see Kidwell, Noley, and Tinker, eds., *A Native American Theology* [Native American theology is a shorthand term for discussing the Native American way of life. See Tinker, *Spirit and Resistance*, 110, but his whole book is highly recommended, and see Tinker's *American Indian Liberation*]. Also see Robin Wall Kimmerer's books *Gathering Moss* and *Braiding Sweetgrass*; and Abram, *Becoming Animal*, 149–50). *Elohim* values this development as good (specifically very good) for its purpose; and again the day's work is ended and night comes. Here we see again that the narrative (and thus all the following biblical canon) should not be interpreted in anthropocentric ways (we have also seen a web of relationships in which *Elohim* is central). The narrative begins with *Elohim* in the first verse, and here in v. 31 we have *Elohim*'s ultimate valuing—the creation is very good for its purposes. And the following in vv. 2:1–4a centers the creation around *Elohim*. But there is still one more day. The poem/narrative of chapter 1 extends through v. 2:4a, which ends the first narrative and serves as a transition to the second narrative while v. 4b introduces the second narrative. LeFebvre also rightly observes a doubling of the evaluation "good" in 1:31 which emphasizes creations' fruitfulness (*The Liturgy of Creation*, 142–45). Creation is very good, but still not perfect. The first creation account also notes that creation is both of materiality (place) and time. The life of the material world is broken up into six days of creation (or work) and one day of rest. Creation isn't complete without *Elohim*'s rest.

Verses 2:1–4a end the first creation story and serves as a transition to the following narrative, and v. 4b begins the second narrative. Genesis 2:1 recognizes that the works of the previous six days of the first creation narrative are completed and continues by observing a seventh day in 2:2 (at least part of the importance behind these verses is to indicate that even given the importance of day 6's length of reporting, and its events, it still is not seen or understood as the high point of creation). The crescendo of creation is day 7. It, more than any other day, is *Elohim*'s day as *Elohim* rests (mystery, and perhaps is better understood as *Elohim* relaxing or contemplating the goodness of the finished work of creation) because *Elohim* recognizes both creations' completion (not perfection), and that it is very good for its purpose (for it can continue creation without *Elohim*'s direct intervention). This confirms that *Elohim* takes up residence in the creation (and yet it seems to not simply be a full or complete residence of Elohim for there is still a part of *Elohim* that is above, or beyond, creation) with the expectation that humans will also care in *Elohim*'s way for creation, and this repeats the original blessing of 1:4 (and gives it even more significance. Creation is very good, but still not perfect). This day is declared as hallowed. This is the only day specifically described as holy, therefore *Elohim*'s day (and is chapter 1's crescendo). As Fretheim observes, "The creational being and becoming is well ordered, but the world does not run like a machine, with a tight casual weave; it has elements of randomness and chaos, of strangeness and wildness. Amid the order there is room for chance (Another mystery)" (*God and the World*, 244).

Chapter 2

THE SECOND CREATION STORY
Act 1: Gen 2:4b–25

As noted above I understand v. 4 (along with the general consensus) is both the end to the first creation story (v. 4a) and the beginning of the second creation story (v. 4b). *Elohim* begins the actual work of creation in the second creation narrative in v. 7. This following narrative seems like, and is, a more primitive account than the first poem/narrative of chapters 1—2:4a.

Verse 5 notes that there was no (this "no" in v. 5 indicates that whatever happens to be is in a negative state) plant in the earth (yet the earth already existed before *YHWH Elohim* begins to create. See Westermann, *Creation*, 74), and that no vegetation was in the field (not the garden) for *Elohim YHWH* (the text actually has *YHWH Elohim* but I understand that *Elohim* is to influence *YHWH* rather than *YHWH* as having the dominating influence over *Elohim*) had not caused it to rain, and there was no human to till (care for) the ground (this also notices that humans are as important to created life as is water, and this looks forward to the vocation/task [the Lord] *Elohim* [God] gives the human in v. 15). However, v. 6 notes that a mist went up to water the ground (this notes the importance that water has in creation, and this may also recognize the place of water in the deep void in 1:2). It was only after the mist first appeared in v. 6 that the verse continues by noting in v. 7 the first act of the Lord *Elohim*. *Elohim* formed the human from the dust of the ground breathing in the breath of life, specifically in the human (*n'shamah hayya*, "living being," is what makes a human human. It was developed later as the Hebrew concept of the *nephesh*. The *nephesh* is the closest the Hebrew comes to the Hellenistic concept of the soul, but the *nephesh* is an expanded version of the self. It might be best to think in terms of the spirit), and this pictures not only the Lord *Elohim*'s intimate presence and relationship specifically with humans, but with all creation as observed in the last creation story; and v. 7 also pictures *Elohim YHWH* as the artisan. This *Elohim* is not unlike Melchizedek's God Most High in Gen 14:18 (*El Elyon*, where *El* is short for *Elohim* and *Elyon* is singular; thus combining the plural with the singular). In the next verse *Elohim* blesses Abraham, and Abraham acknowledges this with his *El Shaddai* (the God Most High, maker of heaven and earth). This breath of the God Most High is the *Elohim YHWH* (*El Yahweh*. See Borgman, *Genesis*, 73–74) in Gen 2 linked with the Creator in Gen 1.

Elohim gives the human life (but there is no difference when the *nephesh* [being, person] of the breath is given to animals, cf. 7:22). Verse 8 sees *Elohim* Yahweh placing the human in the garden of Eden (different from the field in v. 5) in the east (the direction from which life and salvation come). Verse 9 then speaks of *Elohim* Yahweh forming every tree (all vegetation?) that is good for food (food in general, not just food for humans), and specifically noting that the tree of life was in the midst of the garden along with the tree of the knowledge of good and evil (both have good fruit, and the tree of the knowledge of good and evil is neutral here—neither good nor bad. It echoes the void in 1:2, mystery. It must also be noted that the prohibitive command is in the garden, and thus establishes the experience of law in the garden).

Verses 10–14 seem to start an aside or paragraph that discusses the rivers that flow out of the garden of Eden, and around it (and strengthens the crucial role that water plays in creation, seen in v. 6). Actually v. 10 talks about the one river that flows out of the garden and then divides into four rivers. The next three verses describe the divided river. The name of the first is the Pishon; it is the one that flows around the whole land of Havela, where there is good gold. Verse 12 continues on to emphasize that the gold is very good, and that other gems (bdellium and onyx) are also there. Verse 13 describes the river Gihon as the one that flows around the whole land of Cush. And v. 14 describes the Tigress, which flows east of Assyria, and just mentions the fourth as the Euphrates. Together these rivers sort of describe a recognizable place, but no exact location is provided. However, it must be noted the role that the number four plays in Jewish numerology (four is the universal number representing the four points of the compass and the four seasons, or all space and all time). So this can represent the whole world (and yet the garden is realized as a specific place).

In v. 15 we see *Elohim* putting the human in the garden of Eden to "till and keep it." We shouldn't rush by these verbs too quickly because it is the best elaboration that describes *Elohim* Yahweh's understanding of the dominion granted in 1:26. The two verbs are *abad* and *shamar*. As Ellen Davis observes the two verbs describe the human vocation/task as one that is to protect the relationships of the beings of creation and to serve them (*Getting Involved With God*, 92; also see Fretheim, *God and World*, 53–54). That is we humans are to maintain the harmony and balance of the original creation. Davis also discusses the love of land that humans are to have for the land in her excellent commentary *Proverbs, Ecclesiastes, and the Songs of Songs* (236–37). These two verbs show how the usual concept of stewardship for the earth is vastly bankrupt. Fretheim also discusses the love of land in this initial vocation/task given humans by *YHWH Elohim* (and see Trible, *God and the Rhetoric of Sexuality*, 85–86). *Abad* and *shamar* depict the priestly quality of serving and protecting the other for the other's benefit (Paul makes the argument in Rom 12:3 that we shouldn't think more highly of ourselves than we ought, but to think of ourselves properly. Though we are priests for creation we are not over creation). Fretheim (*God and World*, 53–54) further says,

> The divine purpose for the human being that is speci-
> fied in 2:15, to "serve" (*abad*) and "protect" (*shamar*) the

> earth (more natural translations of these verbs), specifi-
> cally connects back to 2:5. The tasks outlined in these two
> texts give to the human a responsibility not only for the
> maintenance and preservation of the creation but also
> for intercreational development. . . . [Davis' work *Getting
> Involved with God*, 92 says that the verbs further describe
> that] the human work in the garden are not most fun-
> damentally words drawn from the fields of horticulture
> and agriculture; in fact only rarely are they [so] used. . . .
> They are words that are more primarily related to human
> activity in relationship to God. . . . Davis also points out
> that the verb *keep* is related to the care of the less fortu-
> nate and vulnerable in the [prophetic] sense of "watch
> over" (see Ps 16:1; 17:8; 86:2).

This is certainly at odds with the usual thought concerning dominion (it is *Elohim*'s understanding of dominion, not the
human's which is pictured by the human male and the woman's
dominion in 3:6–7 and Cain's in 4:8). Though the usual translations aren't wrong, their thought is rather anemic. This describes
humanity's vocation/task as being one that serves and protects
creation for its benefit (certainly carrying definite environmental
concerns, but it is even greater in that it captures a good relationship that maintains the balance described in the first chapter: human partnership with *Elohim* and all creation. It is perhaps more
appropriate to think in terms of accomplices as Abram thinks in
his *Becoming Animal*, 131. At this point I must wonder if sin has
more to do with humans not living into, and for, the purpose of
maintaining the responsibilities *Elohim* has given humans for creation than something that just happens to us?). Verse 16 has *Elohim* allowing for the eating from every tree in the garden, but v. 17
continues in presenting *Elohim*'s first (and only) prohibition: "You
shall not eat it [the tree of knowledge of good and evil] for if you
do you shall surely die"; and it is a necessary grace that also allows
for development of human freedom (Fretheim, *Creation, Fall, and
Flood*, 77) as well as developing the plot. Does this prohibition not
also establish law (and that within the garden)? We are not to eat
of the tree of the knowledge of good and evil. Rather than simply

being prohibitive (though it is certainly that) there seems also to be a subtle encouragement (sort of: "You see those two trees in the middle of the garden? Don't eat from the one on the left but do eat from the one on the right"). If the prohibition is transgressed (eating from the wrong tree and not the right tree) then death will be the result (not capital punishment but mortality. One would perhaps assume physical death, and its immediacy, but the passage assumes something other than just physical death's immediacy).

Verse 18 records *Elohim*'s commentary that it is not good for the human to be alone (for *Elohim* seems not to be alone, cf. 1:26, and one must also ask to whom is *Elohim* speaking? This seems to link back to the "let us" in 1:26, and certainly echoes the relational being of the social *Elohim* in the first story). This is the first part of creation valued by *Elohim*, as specifically "not good" (not even the tree of knowledge of good and evil was considered "not good," though prohibited), and it is addressed to the human who represents all humans. It must be noted that *Elohim* understands that here *Elohim* can't be the helper for the human, for the human is a creature, and must therefore receive creaturely help (yet it is *Elohim* who realizes that something must be done to change the "not good" into good). *Elohim* begins to address the problem by creating the animals and bringing them to the human for naming (on the fullest aspect of naming see Fretheim, *The Suffering of God*, 100–101. Though Fretheim is addressing God's naming of the God-self it also applies for the human act of naming, for humans are to be *Elohim*'s image).

In vv. 19–20 *Elohim*, seemingly rather naively, makes the animals from the ground (on second thought, this isn't a naivety; rather, it pictures *Elohim*'s valuing of the animals); and brings them to the human to name (naming gives an identity to their personhood, qualities, and establishes relationship with the one named, but can also designate a certain superiority over the named, though not necessarily. The naming here refers to companionship, not sexuality). The translation of "animal" or "beast" is better translated as "living being" as it is the same word to describe the human in 2:7 (*nephesh* does not mean soul, but addresses the totality of the self, Trible, *God and the Rhetoric of Sexuality*, 145. Also see Westermann where he talks in terms of a living soul, living being, *Creation*, 77–78). Here the human is exercising the given responsibility of dominion, and *Elohim* Yahweh needs to find out how the human will evaluate them (do they both help and fit?). This claiming of evaluating something *Elohim* seems to think will work seems somewhat arrogant by the human, but *Elohim* will abide by the human's evaluation (and humans are the only part of creation given this power of valuing, which is another part of *Elohim*'s image)! This is a self-emptying (*kenosis*) of *Elohim* (still another part of the *Elohim*'s image that is to inform what it means to be created in *Elohim*'s image) that builds upon the kenosis that we've already seen (*Elohim* isn't the only one who can value), and *Elohim* will abide by the human's valuing. So *Elohim* creates the animals and brings them to the human (the phrase translated as "every beast" or "every creature" is best translated as "living be-ing," *nephesh hayyah*), and in v. 20 the human gives the evaluation, and records that the human didn't find any one that truly fulfilled *Elohim*'s intent, or the human's need. Though some animals can be more helpful than others, and one can sort of communicate with some of them more easily than others, one can't fully converse with any of them, fully reason with them, fully partner with them, or fully work with them. This negative evaluation sends *Elohim* back to the drawing board ("I'll have to make something new").

Elohim leaves the valuing up to the human who reports that a "helper/companion was not found to be a fit" (Trible suggests that companion is a better translation of *'ezer*, "helper," *God and the Rhetoric of Sexuality*, 90. It must be realized that one can't be a true companion or partner while one rules over the other. This rul-ing comes later as a result of sin (and the results haven't changed). Fretheim observes that the word "helper" is used primarily in the Older Testament for *Elohim* (see Deut 33:7, 26) who is our helper (Donald Gowan in his *From Eden to Babel*, 45–46 reminds us that in the seventeenth-century English of the KJV, "meet" meant "ap-propriate"). The human is in need of someone to be a representa-tive of God at his side" (*Creation, Fall, and Flood*, 78). *Elohim*'s presence is not enough for the human, and that is recognized by *Elohim*! The text continues by making the further comment that it is to be one that is fit for the human. "Helper" and "fit," though not simply incorrect translations, are, however, rather anemic. It is better understood as a counterpart companion, one who can be in an entire relationship (not just sexual). The emphasis here isn't simply sexual (though that is perhaps also in view); rather, it describes a co-relationship in which one can truly carry on conversation with, reason with, debate with, work with, and be entirely in relation with the other.

Verse 21 picks that creation up with *Elohim* putting the human asleep (or in a deep meditative state, or a prophetic trance) and removes something from the human's side (rib, flesh, muscle, or something else we don't know. Only that it was removed from the human's side, not the head or the feet. Either of those would picture being ruled over, or ruling over, the other); and closes up the place. Verse 22 reports that *Elohim* made a woman (now the human becomes the human male. The Hebrew *adamah* is not yet a personal name, and only becomes so sometime in chapters 4 or 5, debate is still out. So human male is preferred rather than a personal name for there is now a human female that provides the distinction that qualifies the human as a human male). *Elohim* brings her to the human male, and again *Elohim* will abide by the human male's evaluation. Verse 23 gives that human male's evaluation, "This is bone of my bones/ and flesh of my flesh;/ she shall be called Woman ['*issa*], because she was taken out of the human male ['*is* man (sic)]." That is the human male's evaluation. Is there anything explicitly sexual in that? It rather focuses on our common humanness and companionship, not our sexual qualities (see Trible, *God and the Rhetoric of Sexuality*, 12–23, 98–102, where she observes that this is the first time the *adamah* describes itself as man, '*is*). Now hear the narrator's comment in v. 24: "Therefore a man [*sic*] will leave his father and mother and cleave to his wife and they become one flesh." That is the narrator's evaluation, and it is somewhat sexual (for marriage in that culture expected sexual relations, though it must be noted that this evaluating does not address the bearing of children. It does address the relationship between a human male and a woman), but it is not *Elohim*'s, or the human male's, evaluation. Verse 25 continues by saying that the human male and the woman (the narrator again says wife) were both naked and were not ashamed. The narrator's evaluation is seen by some to sexualize the human male's evaluation, and yet here it speaks more of a child's innocence than the life of an adult human. This also represents the creation of social ordering (here familial, but later also national [Gen 10–11] and cultural [Gen 4]; Fretheim, *God and the World*, 6).

Trible argues that Eros (a good garden of harmony), its pleasures and worship in v. 8; its delights in vv. 9 and 16; the noticing of the need for companions in v. 18; the creation of eroticism proper in vv. 21–22; and the human male's evaluation of that creation in v. 23 were all part of *Elohim*'s good creation. And chapter 3 uncreates it, turning it into a bent desire (*God and the Rhetoric of Sexuality*, 72–143)

THE SECOND CREATION STORY

Act 2: Gen 3:1–24

Genesis 3 opens by introducing a serpent (the serpent was worshiped as a symbol of deity in Canaanite religion which often seduced Israel, Fretheim, *Creation, Fall, and Flood*, 82. And Gowan, *From Eden to Babel*, 51, notes a play on the words *'arum*, "naked," in 2:25 and *'arummim*, "subtle" or "clever," and this word pair again appears in vv. 6–7). The serpent is crafty, more so than any other creature (perhaps because the serpent/snake can sneak up silently). One must first note that this serpent is a creature and therefore has a rightful place in the garden (the woman is not pictured as surprised, startled, or in any way intimidated by the serpent's presence in the garden). The serpent's question is specifically asked of both the human male and the woman about the possibility of eating of any tree in the garden. The "you" in v. 1 is understood to be plural and so indicates that the human male is present, but it is the woman who answers in vv. 2–3. In v. 4, the "you" is singular. In v. 2 it is the woman who responds, saying, "We may eat of the fruit of the trees of the garden" (the "we" includes the human male with the woman), and she goes on to expand the prohibition in v. 3 saying, "but God said, 'You shall not eat of any of the fruit of the tree which is in the midst of the garden, neither shall you touch it, lest you die.'" Now it must be noted that this also means to not even eat of the tree of life (whose presence the woman doesn't acknowledge in v. 3), which was also in the midst of the garden. Nor should they even go so close as to touch the tree of knowledge of good and evil, or the tree of life. The serpent responds in v. 4, but specifically to the woman, "You [singular] will not die" (which is somewhat true, for neither the woman the human male or the woman die immediately). The serpent continues in v. 5, "For God knows that when you [plural] eat of it your [plural] eyes will be opened, and you [plural] will be like God, knowing good and evil." The serpent's voice changes from the singular you used in specifically addressing the woman in v. 4 to the plural voice in v. 5 because the serpent is addressing both the woman and the human male (who has been present during the whole scene). Perhaps the human male doesn't correct the woman's elaboration on the prohibition because he shares it. There is an important difference between the woman's "lest you die" in 3:3 and *Elohim*'s prohibition in 2:17, "you shall surely die," and must be noted. It is the difference between the understanding of capital punishment (between the woman's "lest") and *Elohim*'s "you shall," denoting mortality (a re-affirmation of their already existing mortality, see Fretheim, *Genesis*, 352). Perhaps the human male's lack of correction (maybe he shares the woman's understanding) urges the serpent on? Or perhaps the human male just goes quiet out of intimidation. In any case the plural "you" should be translated as "you all" in vv. 1 and 5. The "knows" in v. 5 implies that *Elohim* has not shared the whole truth (and the serpent didn't also). Can *Elohim*, who has withheld something that seems good, be entirely trusted? Verse 6 records the woman's reasoning and response (the end of the verse implies that the human male is present in the scene. The human male, having gone quiet, does not respond to the serpent, and doesn't correct the woman. Nor does she seek his advice, and neither the woman nor the human male consult one another or *Elohim*. This is an individualistic act of pride which Rom 12:3 rightly questions). She makes up her mind by herself, and the human male lets her (both violate *Elohim*'s assessment that it is not good for humans to be alone and independent [an individual is a political concept, not a created concept]. Each of them respond out of their own decisions made with no consultation with *any* other). She sees that, like other fruit, it is good for food, and that it is delightful to see. She also realized that it is to be desired for the purpose of making one wise. This is not at all bad. Good fruit to eat, delightful to see, and the wisdom literature spends much time noting that the effort and labor of seeking wisdom is much to be desired. However, this story asks whether it is good to achieve wisdom according to *my* own schedule, and by *my* own means, or *Elohim*'s? Essentially the problem is about who to trust, oneself or *Elohim* (I understand this as the only dualism appropriate in Gen 1–11). Westermann puts it in terms of a desire to master one's own existence *Genesis 1–11* (247–48; cf. *Elohim*'s encouragement to Cain in 4:7 and the Babel builders desire to make a name for themselves in 11:4). Tertullian understood this lack of trust or desire as impatience, and impatience as the original sin (see Krieder, *The Patient Ferment of the Early Church*, 22). The woman eats, and also gives some to the human male, and he eats (this emphasizes that it was the human male's choice, his free choice). The interesting thing is that this ability to have a free choice images *Elohim* who can freely choose whether to create or not, and how. That *Elohim* chooses to create in a way that has to take account of that creation and react to/ with it is *Elohim*'s choice and is meant to influence humans as we interact with creation. This ability to choose images *Elohim*, but the decision of the choice does not necessarily image *Elohim*, for the decision is ours.

The following emphasis in v. 7 goes on to say that their eyes were opened (this must have been somewhat of a shock, being naked in front of others and realizing it for the first time!). I can of course speak into other dimensions of nakedness, but the following verse has them making aprons out of fig leaves to cover their physical nakedness. I have not found anyone mentioning the irony in v. 7 that seems so evident to me (though my study is certainly not exhaustive). Back in 2:15 we discussed the pastoral qualities inherent in *Elohim*'s vocation/task given to humans, and it has not been changed (except by the humans!). There we saw that the original vocation/task given humans was/is to serve and protect creation, and that for its benefit. Here we see the humans changing that vocation/task by making creation (pictured in the fig leaves) serve them, and in such a way as to offer some protection. Does the irony really escape anyone? This also is the initial occurrence of an anthropocentric arrogance (humans thinking that they are so much better than the rest of creation that creation is therefore meant to serve us).

Fretheim offers a good summary about the thought concerning original sin (*God and the World*, 70–71). He says,

> This link (on the thoughts between 3:1–24 and 4:7–16) should be extended through 6:1–5, where the cosmic effects of sin are mythically conveyed with 6:5 summarizing the situation at that juncture, namely the universality and inevitability of human sinfulness. No such claim is made at the end of chapter 3. . . . Rather, chapter 3 describes the "originating sin," and the chapters that follow speak of a *process* by which sin becomes "original" that is universal and inescapable (no genetic understandings are conveyed).

Verses 8–19 start by having *Elohim* walking in the garden, actually the Hebrew says, "in the *midst* [*betook*] of the garden" (Trible, *God and the Rhetoric of Sexuality*, 117). This is the same place that the disobedience occurred. *Elohim* walks in the cool of the day, and the human male and the woman hide themselves from *Elohim*'s presence. This is a new thing, this hiding (or the attempt to hide from *Elohim*), a typical human response. In v. 9 *Elohim* calls to the human male. "Where are you?" This initially seems to be a naive question from *Elohim*. For how can anyone/anything hide from *Elohim*'s presence? In the first creation narrative we saw *Elohim*'s intimate presence with all creation, and this presence was affirmed in the second creation narrative. On second thought this is actually *Elohim* giving the human male the opportunity to own up to what the human male has done.

Verse 10 has the human male responding that he heard *Elohim* walking in the garden and confesses his fear (this fear is pointed at *Elohim though* it is a common fear of all humanity: the fear of not measuring up, but nonetheless trying to overcome that fear through our own means) because he was naked, "so I hid" (a common human response, and this is a self-centered attempt to justify and rationalize oneself. This self-centered individuality gets developed further through, at least, in chapter 4). In v. 11 *Elohim* asks the human male, "Who told you that you were naked? Have you eaten of the tree I commanded you not to eat?" In v. 12 the human male still doesn't own his act but passes it on to the woman (the harmonious unity of one flesh of 2:23 is now one that is confrontational, turning the human male against the woman. This is the development of misogamy, and it is because of sin). In v. 13 *Elohim* confronts the woman, "What have you done?" No trickery is mentioned by *Elohim*, neither does she accuse God as the male did by his saying, "It is you that gave me the woman"; this also denies the human male's valuation in 2:23. The human male blames *Elohim* in 3:12. And the woman also refuses to own her act and passes it on to the serpent. *YHWH Elohim* confronts the serpent (who, as animal, does not share the same dignity that humans have, although his worth before *Elohim* is the same; and he does share in the results of the event as the web of relations demands). This is the order of creation, what affects one part affects all, and shows that not only do the nonhuman creatures share in the creative powers they also share in the uncreative powers, cf. 6:7. Now a moral dimension is added to the created order. By moral dimension I mean that the morality in *Elohim*'s created order is subjected to the moral order of human choice. In this section *Elohim* spells out just how sin affects the creation (sin isn't mentioned in the first 3 chapters). Sin isn't something *Elohim* created, it comes from human choices, and only enters creation through those choices. Bruce Birch describes sin well as, "Do we answer experiences where we feel wronged by further wronging another? Cain [humans in general] has the ability to make moral choices that restore or further break relationships" ("Creation and the Moral Development of God in Genesis 1–11," in Gaiser and Throntveit, eds., *"And God Saw That It Was Good"*, 18). *Elohim* acknowledges that "Because you [the serpen] have done this, cursed are you above all cattle, and wild animals." There is now a curse, but *Elohim* merely pronounces that the serpent is now cursed; *Elohim* did not specifically curse the serpent (apparently the curse comes from a violation of the created order and not directly from *Elohim*. *Elohim* did nonetheless create the created order the way it is and so is somewhat implicated in the curse. Gen 5:29 states, in addition, that *Elohim* cursed the ground, and shows that *Elohim* was/is always vulnerably implied in a violation of the created order, and so is implicated in its curse).

It must be understood that the following verses are not curses and are only descriptive of life; and are not simply formative for life in this world. Punishment is reserved for expulsion from the garden, not simply for life lived in this world. The serpent's curse is that "now you shall go upon your belly, all the days of your life. I will put enmity between you and the woman, and between your seed and her seed; [her seed] shall bruise your head, and [your seed] shall bruise [her seed's] heel." The first thing to notice is the cursing. *Elohim* pronounces the curse to the serpent in v. 14, but not the woman or the human male, and only announces that the ground is now cursed as a result of the human male's choice (*Elohim* does not curse either the ground or the human male. Instead *Elohim* announces that now the ground is cursed as a consequence, which not only affects the human male, but also everything else in creation, as the web of relationships demand). The second thing concerns the seed (both the serpent's and the woman's seed). The seed is plural in the sense that it includes all snakes and all humans. The ending of v. 15 has the woman (and her seed) bruising the serpent's head, and the serpent (and his seed) bruising the woman's heel (this pictures their enmity, and that it is specifically caused or allowed by *Elohim*).

In v. 16 *Elohim* focuses on the woman, saying, "I will greatly multiply your pain in childbearing; in pain you shall bring forth children, yet your desire shall be for your husband, and he shall rule over you" (this is the price she pays: a price not only of increased pain in childbirth, but also of the "husband" ruling over the woman, and yet she will still long for the relationship). Here in v. 16 *Elohim* does not accuse the woman like in the accusations against the serpent, and the human male in v. 17 (Trible, *God and the Rhetoric of Sexuality*, 126). A couple of things: the pain was increased, and not appearing for the first time (so there was pain in the garden before chapter 3, and the suffering that results from it), and the human male never ruled over the woman in the garden until now (it is the result of the originating sin and remains so).

In vv. 17–19 *Elohim* addresses the human male, saying,

> Because you have listened to the voice of your wife, and have eaten of the tree of which I commanded you, "You shall not to eat of it," cursed is the ground because of you; in toil you shall eat of it all the days of your life; thorns and thistles it shall bring forth to you; and you shall eat the plants of the field. In the sweat of your face you shall eat bread till you return to the ground, for out of it you were taken; and to dust you shall return.

Listening to the voice of your wife doesn't mean that the human male is so above the woman that he shouldn't ever listen to her or consult her (we saw in 2:18 that it is not good for humans to be alone, to be independent, or to decide on their own, and *Elohim*'s following work intends to turn the "not good" into good). It means that the human male did not correct the woman's elaboration of the prohibition, and just stayed silent (this need for discernment into situations is also part of "not being alone," and is certainly a necessity required in the performance of our vocation/task). *Elohim* reaffirms the correct commandment concerning the prohibition in 17b, and simply announces that the ground is now cursed (not the human male—it is sort of like this: "The ground is now hurt and I must allow this as my order of creation dictates [this "subduing," not *Elohim*'s dominion, is because of the human choice in 3:1–7, and remains abundantly evident in humans today]. In any case I allow the ground to curse you for it curses you; but I will not curse you. The ground curses you, and that for your infraction." The original vocation/task given shall now be one of toil (enmity from the ground), yet the humans shall continue to use vegetation life for food. In v. 18 *Elohim* continues to elaborate on the infraction, saying, "thorns and thistles [the ground] shall bring forth to you. . . . In the sweat of your face you shall eat bread till you return to the ground; for out of it you were taken; you are dust, and to dust you shall return [we find out here that this death was not a capital punishment, but this death of mortality is also a grace of *Elohim*. For who would want to live forever in a world subjected to the above sentence?]." The ground shall now produce thorns and thistles and will not simply be the overabundant fruitfulness creation was intended to be, for it is now cursed as a result of the human's choice. The humans were to maintain creation's fruitfulness, and now it shall be toilsome labor! We are dust (this does not mean that humans now have no dignity before *Elohim*. It is a description, and reminder, of our creation, and that we are now mortal. That we were taken from the dust, and to dust we shall return.) It seems to me that the description the passage presents is one where inheritance of sin is not through the parentage of the human male and the woman but through the changes that their choice (their wrongful subduing of creation) and its effects have brought on creation. This emphasizes that we will experience physical death, and not just toilsome work, or the pain of labor and the breaking of relationships. As Birch et al. say, "Modern physics (quantum mechanics, chaos theory) has helped us see that this is not a closed system of cause and effect; there is a loose, if complex, casual weave or 'play' within God's design that makes novelty, freshness, surprise, and serendipity possible (see Job 38–41)" (*A Theological Introduction to the Old Testament*, 271).

In v. 20 the human male names the woman Eve (the Hebrew name resembles living, and this naming echoes the naming of the animals in 2:19–20). Then in v. 21 we find the grace of *Elohim* (which shows that *Elohim* still treats the humans with dignity). *Elohim* forms more appropriate garments for the humans that will better stand up to the hard labor the humans will now have in order to live (this is a reaffirmation of human dignity and pictures the judgment of affirmation). However, the end of v. 19 affirms that the life will end in death, as *Elohim* said in 2:17.

Verses 22–23 is an interesting passage, and the usual translations don't really know what to do with it. Verse 22 has *Elohim* musing over the concern that the humans may also possibly eat of the tree of life, and so live forever (this is also *Elohim*'s grace, because who would want to live forever under the conditions spelled out above?). And perhaps *Elohim*'s musings are not simply just internal musings (are they also before all creation and the council of the gods?). *Elohim*'s musings affirm the serpent's questioning of one's trust in *Elohim*. That being "humans have become like us knowing good and evil." Then the end of v. 22 is the part that translators don't really know how to handle. It is either rendered as "..." or "—" because the end of the verse is a pause. However, some scholars see that as a way the early Hebrew expressed deep emotion (John C. Collins, *Genesis 1–4*, 175). If we think into this contemplation by *Elohim* we can perhaps think into *Elohim*'s reasoning: "I really wanted the humans to stay in my garden and care for it, but now it seems I must think of a way of keeping the humans from the tree of life. I will have to suffer expelling them from the garden." Fretheim observes that suffering may indeed become a vocation saying, "Indeed, suffering may become a vocation for us because it is a vocation for God.: suffering is God's chief way of being powerful in the world (cf. Is. 1:2–4, cf. Phil. 2:1–11)." This is part of the image we were created into and also are to image. If that is the case then here in vv. 22–23 we have a picture of a good parent responding to a child who has just done something that they (just previously) were warned not to do. The act may indeed produce anger, but a good parent doesn't simply express that anger ("Ooo, now I hate you!"); rather, that parent's anger would be expressed as suffering in the in deep disappointment ("I wish you hadn't done that. Didn't I just tell you not to do it? But now . . ."). And that understanding fits better in the story told in 2:4b—3:24.

Fretheim observes that "The God-ward side of wrath and judgment is grief (and the God-ward side of woe is alas). For God, an internal grieving always accompanies wrath and judgment (as is commonly the case in the breakdown of inter-human relationships," *Jeremiah*, 603). Fretheim observes in Jeremiah's oracle against Moab (certainly not a chosen people) that God's grief is similar to God's grief over the judgment and destruction of Israel. And he also compares God's grief and lamentation for Moab as being similar to the grief and lamentation over the judgment and destruction of Israel (*Jeremiah*, 355–605). This is the same grief that the space between vv. 22–23 captures.

Verse 23 follows up by having the narrator, not *Elohim*, finishing *Elohim*'s musing, and follows in v. 24 by explaining that, "therefore *Elohim* sent humanity east from the garden of Eden and placed a cherubim . . . to guard the way to the tree of life with a flaming sword protecting the way to the tree of life," John Walton observes that the cherubim's Older Testament's function were as guardians of God's presence (Walton, *Genesis*, 230). So here the tree of life is equated with *Elohim*'s life. They are not just protecting the way into the garden, but to *Elohim*, which is depicted here as the tree of life (this also seems to establish a separation between the highest heaven [the celestial realm of *Elohim*] and the lower heavens or the sky and the outer space, of this creation). The garden, the tree of life, and the highest heaven now seem for humanity to be non-reachable essence, but that unreachablity is specifically regarding the tree of life, the full presence of *Elohim*, who now seems to be a hidden this-worldly presence.

Chapter 3 does not call the serpent Satan "evil," or demonizes the serpent in any way (neither does Gen 1–11, or Genesis as a whole. Indeed the serpent seems to be the perennial trickster but the teaching quality that the trickster has for Native Americans must be noted). And the Hebrew word for sin does not occur in chapter 3. Whatever happened to sin? The word first occurs in 4:7 in the Cain and Abel story. Indeed, chapter 3 does not really picture a fall at all as in the common thought. Westermann observed that "The teaching of the fall and of original sin rests [in a] late Jewish interpretation (Esdras 7:118). It has no foundation at all in the narrative" (*Creation*, 108). Daniel Shroyer understands chapter 3 as being similar to a coming of age story (*Original Blessing*), and it does bear many similarities. In any case it doesn't change at all the original blessing. It does, however, present a movement from the garden to the world as we know and experience it. It is a narrative that still pictures both the human male and the woman with dignity. And is another picture of kenosis (self-emptying) that we see of *Elohim*. "*Adama* and Eve, what you've done seriously impacts all creation (a violation of creation's order affects cosmic order, which is a redundant statement, cf. 6:1–4), and has its ramifications; but it is still not a deal breaker with me. I will continue to be in relationship with you and be present to you."

It must also be emphasized that the rest of the Older Testament does not refer to the happenings in chapter 3 (with the possible exception of Ezek 28:1–19), but since we're still in the opening chapter of the OT (that being Gen 1–11) chapter 3 still has an important informing value over the rest of the scriptural canon.

It must be emphasized that chapter 3 is the second half of chapter 2, it is part of the same narrative and should not be separated from chapter 2 just as chapter 2 should not be separated from chapter 1. I must also restate my suggestion that *YHWH* from Gen 2 on must be informed by the *Elohim* tradition of chapter 1. Hence my emphasis of *Elohim*.

GEN 4 AND 5

GENESIS 4

Chapter 4 starts with the Cain and Abel story. In v. 1 we have the first account of the human sexual act (and that outside of the garden! Was there any human sexual activity inside the garden, and how long were the humans in the garden anyway?). "The human male knew Eve, and she conceived." The Hebrew turns a word into a personal name by dropping the definite article. Verse 4:25 is the first time this appears (others argue for 5:1 as the first time Adam becomes a personal name). Eve rejoices at Cain's birth saying, "I have purchased [usual translations say "gotten"] a man [*sic*] with the help of *Elohim*." Fretheim observes that the word translated above as "purchased" is now preferred by scholars as is shown in other Near Eastern texts. He observes that the saying by Eve refers to the price/difficulty in the bearing of children (cf. 3:16, *Creation, Fall, and Flood*, 95). In any case this statement is surprising. The surprise isn't in "gotten" or "purchase." The surprise is in Eve's wording of "man," not baby or child. Is this a one-ups man-ship by Eve over the human male in Eve's thinking in essentially saying, "Yes you rule over me, but I create with *Elohim*'s help")? In v. 2 we see her again bearing his brother (and contains no such excited expression). He was named Abel (the name is descriptive of Eve's lack of excitement and refers to the nothingness of vapor. With no excitement at Abel's birth, like at Cain's birth, his name seems to appropriately describe his lack of importance to Eve). The verse also describes Abel as a keeper of sheep and Cain as a tiller of the ground. Now it seems that Cain continues most explicitly keeps the original vocation given in 2:15, but Abel expresses that particularly in keeping sheep (also part of creation and therefore part of the original vocation/task too). But Abel's practice is the only one highlighted in Heb 11:4 (which observes his faith. It should be noted that this is the faith of a non or pre-Israelite, they also can have faith). However, in v. 4, Cain is the first to offer a sacrifice, and that by a non/pre-Israelite (Cain and Abel's faith is pre-Israelite). The sacrifice is not a sacrifice for salvation, but a sacrifice of thanksgiving for creation, yet Cain must be disrespected even though he is the first to offer sacrifice (is this *Elohim*'s testing of Cain?). In *The Chalice and the Blade* Riane Eisler offers an interesting reason why the serpent, and the woman in chapter 3; and Cain, along with agricultural work in chapter 4, must all be discredited. She observes that the cultures of old Europe (European cultures before the steppe invasions from Russia. Does this also apply to Palestine before the nomadic pastoral Semitic invaders?) were more equal in the sharing of power and authority between the sexes than Western cultures after the steppe invasions, with authority probably leaning a little toward women. They were also largely agrarian. And an important symbol was the snake, though the butterfly also had some importance, but the snake more because rather than seeming to come back to life only once (like the metamorphosis of the butterfly) the snake was seen as coming back to life several times (in the shedding of his skin). The snake sheds his skin several times during the growing season, and it also goes dormant during the colder months; and comes back to life in the spring when it warms up. And these cultures were seen as matriarchal cultures (anything that is not specifically patriarchal is unfairly seen by the patriarchal cultures as matriarchal, which is seen unfairly as women dominating men), and so those cultures must be discredited by the incoming patriarchal, and pastoral cultures (hence, the discrediting of the snake, women, and agriculture). But it is at least as important to note that the snake was also a divine image in Canaanite religion.

In v. 4 *Elohim* has regard for Abel's offering, but not for Cain's offering (no reason given. Is this also part of the test?). Here I must include some explanation of Daniel Quinn's provocative novel *Ishmael* (173–74) as it offers an interesting solution concerning the choice of Abel over Cain, though I read it after I wrote this study. Quinn's novel compares the cultures developed by the takers (the settled agricultural system that dominates the world that we call "civilized") versus the leavers (semi-nomadic hunter/gatherer cultures that are semi-agricultural that our culture calls "primitive"). Quinn understands the story to be Semitic warfare propaganda against the "civilized" takers (I think this is the best explanation I've heard concerning the choice of the story). Quinn describes his philosophy as "New Tribalism," and so Cain's countenance falls as he becomes angry. In v. 6 *Elohim* questions Cain's response, "Why are you angry, and why has your countenance fallen?" and encourages Cain, "If you do well, will you not be accepted? And if you do not do well, sin is crouching at the door; and its desire [see Ellen Davis' discussion where she notes that the Hebrew word *teshuqah* (desire) appears only three times (Gen 3:16; Gen 4:7; and in the Song of Songs 7:10), *Proverbs, Ecclesiastes, and the Song of Songs*, 294–95] is for you, but you must master it." Several things must be noted. It is anger that is considered not being accepted (that which is not well, and Fretheim observes that "anger is not an attribute of God either, but is a contingent response" [*Jeremiah*, 355]. The humans have now imaged anger, not *Elohim*). This is the first mention of the Hebrew word for sin, and sin is pictured as having an enticing and possessive character, and its own purpose. This mirrors what happened in chapter 3. The snake has, in my estimation, wrongly been linked with sin; and has become its representative (but we noted sin is a result of human choice and can't therefore be relegated to "The devil made me do it"). Sin is at the door and its desire is for us. But *Elohim* doesn't simply command Cain to control sin (it's evident that he/we can't), but that's what the usual translation to "master" suggests. The problem of the individual is also further developed here. The problem is seen between the individual and the community—the web of relationships or the individual (but it is not good for humans to be alone, simply an individual. Rather, this speaks of a radically different way of being that chooses the benefit of the community over one's own individual benefit. It understands that an individual's benefit ultimately rests in the community—the web of relationships). This narrative develops the individual problem by developing the ego (a protection of an independent response). Cain's ego doesn't really allow himself to be questioned by *Elohim*. Westermann observes that v. 7 is a difficult verse to translate and understand (*Genesis 1–11*, 299–301). He observes that the command in the verse is to Cain and is a warning to Cain that he must master it (that Cain must not be mastered by sin). This is somewhat removed from simply mastering it. He conjectures that a better translation is, "But you [Cain], will you master it?" Steinbeck in *East of Eden* does a good job in calling the usual translation ("you must master it") into question. He suggests that the phrase can also mean, "you may master it." And in adding Westermann's suggestion to Steinbeck's one sees a subtle encouragement by *Elohim* for Cain not to be mastered by sin: "Cain, you may master it ("Come on Cain, you can avoid being mastered by it"). Both these translations fit the story (and Gen 4–11) much better.

Verse 8 gives Cain's decided response (we again hear of no consultation with any other; neither human, *Elohim*, nor any other part of creation; again an individual pursuit). And we again have another pause where Cain asks Abel to go out to the field. . . pause. Then it takes up with them going out to the field. Many have wondered what do we miss in the pause? Perhaps what we miss, if our treatment of 3:22–23 is correct, that the pause in ancient Hebrew expresses deep emotion; then it is a picture of Cain wrestling with the idea of killing Abel. But Cain is of coarse overcome with the temptation. Cain designs a plan to get Abel out to a field where he murders Abel. In v. 9 *Elohim* confronts Cain, "Where is your brother?" Again this doesn't address a naivety in *Elohim*, rather it is *Elohim*'s mercy offered Cain by offering Cain a chance of owning up to what he has done. To which Cain responds, "I did not know; am I my brother's keeper?" Here we see Cain's denial of *Elohim*'s question, an ego development in denying any responsibility for his brother. Of coarse, given the relational requirements developed in chapter 1, he is. In v. 10 *Elohim* further questions Cain (*Elohim* isn't satisfied with Cain's response), "What have you done? The voice of your brother's blood is crying from the ground (the ground itself testifies against Cain. This decision of Cain to kill his brother bears similarly to Aeschylus's informative trilogy play *Orestia* that provides the reason for the change from the millennial forms of matriarchal civilizations of some 60,000 years to a domineering patriarchal civilization of some 10,000 years, Eisler *Chalice & the Blade*, 79–82)." In v. 11 *Elohim* pronounces Cain's cursing, "And now you are cursed from the ground, which has opened its mouth to receive your brother's blood from your hand," (acts that break relationships have consequences). *Elohim* doesn't curse Cain, or the ground. *Elohim* just pronounces that Cain is cursed from the ground by emphasizing that it is, "from your hand" (Cain is responsible for the curse). *Elohim* doesn't curse Cain (or the ground), but simply affirms the ground's curse. Sort of, "I didn't want this, but now the result is that you are cursed from the ground. It vomits you out for making it drink your brother's blood (the ground testifies against Cain and the result is that Cain is cursed because of his actions. Violation of the cosmic order violates, or curses, the violator as well as the cosmic order)." *Elohim* continues to explain the implications of the curse in v. 12, "When you till the ground it shall no longer yield to you its strength (apparently it has in spite of the ground's curse in 3:17. This seems to be of the realm of magic), and as a result, "you shall be a fugitive and a wander on the earth." In v. 13 Cain responds, "My punishment is more than I can bear. Behold You have driven me away this day from the ground (Cain doesn't accept his responsibility for the curse, he rather blames *Elohim*); and from Your face I shall be hidden; and a wander on the earth, and whoever finds me will slay me (Cain will now be a stranger to all, and therefore below all; so then the fear of being killed by any one else is appropriate)." *Elohim* responds, "Not so! If anyone slays Cain, vengeance shall be taken sevenfold." This affirms creational law in both its negative terms (2:15–17) and its positive terms in *Elohim*'s ordering of, and interaction with, creation in 1:26–28 (Fretheim, *God and the World*, 135). And *Elohim* put a mark on Cain, lest anyone who came upon him should kill him. "Not so!" In other words I have not driven you from My face or the ground, because you did that; and you shall not be hidden from Me. And yes, you are cursed for the ground has removed its strength from you; but I put a mark on you to protect you." In v. 16 Cain leaves the presence of *Elohim* (not only does Cain refuse to be questioned by *Elohim*, Cain doesn't even want to be anywhere near *Elohim*) and dwells in the land of Nod, which is east of Eden.

A couple of things: one is that it is specifically Cain who leaves the presence of *Elohim*, not *Elohim* from Cain (who still chooses to be present to Cain; it must also be noted that this story is about religious differences; Fretheim, *Genesis*, 377). It is also another picture of kenosis in Gen 1–11. In other words, "Cain, though what you did changes things, and has its serious implications for you; it is still not a deal breaker with me (even though broken relationships have their consequences they do not overcome *Elohim*'s grace. *Elohim* graciously marks Cain). I will be in relationship with you, and be present with you, and protect you even though you choose to leave me." The second thing to note is that Nod (which means wandering, and those who follow Cain's lead are wanderers) is east of Eden, the place from which salvation and life come (not that salvation and life come from Nod, but because of its being in the east it is among the first to receive salvation and life).

The narrative in vv. 17–24 is the first genealogy we have and addresses cultural development (it must be noted that not all cultural developments are good, or bad; and it must also be noted that the genealogies in vv. 17–22 speak of the human fulfillment of the command to multiply. But it seems that humans have been too successful in following that part of the command to the harm of the rest of creation, and we have not necessarily been fruitful).

Now we get the first genealogy, and this genealogy starts with Cain in v. 17. Though the human male is mentioned in the first verse (commonly named Adam, but Adam doesn't become a name until v. 25 or later) it is striking that this genealogy does indeed begin with Cain, and not the human male. Cain knows his wife and she conceived and bore Enoch. This implies that the human male and Eve are representatives of a larger human population, for where did Cain get his wife? Cain builds the first city which he names after his son (why a city for only 5 people? This is further evidence that the human male, Eve, and Cain are representative of a group of people). Jacques Ellul, in his *The Meaning of the City*, notes that the city is the first and the pre-eminent act of human creation. The city is a place where Cain, and his followers, can obtain protection, security, and comfort separate from *Elohim*. However, Ellul only refers to the city in the negative, which is too shortsighted for God later reclaims culture through Seth's genealogy, and the city in Jerusalem. In v. 18 the genealogy progresses simply, "To Enoch was born Irad; and Irad was the father of Me-hu'jael; and Me-hu'jael was the father of Me-thusha-el; and Me-thusha-el was the father of Lamech. Verse 19 notes an importance to Lamech by noting his wives (he had two wives Adah and Zillah). This is the first mention of a man having multiple wives as well as the mentioning of women (this seems to be a further discrediting of women by linking women with Lamech's evil) but it also looks forward to a goodness in the cultural development of vv. 20–23. For the following verses also describe a goodness coming from Adah and Zillah (in spite of the bad qualities that Cain projects on his linage). Verse 20 notes that Adah bore Jabal who was the father of all who dwell in tents and have cattle. Verse 21 talks about his brother who was Jubal. He was the father of those who play the lyre and the pipe. Verse 22 notes that Zillah bore Tubal-cain who was the forger of all instruments of bronze and iron, and just mentions his sister Na'amah (why? perhaps because Tubal-cain didn't have a brother). Verse 23 backtracks to Lamech and his wives. It is a short poem where he talks to his wives (which seems a good thing), but it is a boast about the slaying of a human, and a young man (23b RSV). Borgman in his *Genesis: The Story We Haven't Heard* (34) refers to a boy in 23c while the Tanakh (Gen 4:23 refers to a lad. The RSV's "young man" is too easily assumed to be the human mentioned earlier in 23b). In other words Lamech's boast is, "Not only have I killed a man, but I've also killed a boy/lad for just hurting me." Verse 24 ends the poem in noting that, "if Cain was avenged sevenfold, then I will be avenged seventy-sevenfold." The number seven addresses the completion of seven days, so seven squared is a serious addition to that; and that by Lemech (which stands in opposition to *Elohim* by echoing *Elohim*'s treatment of Cain in 4:15)!

In vv. 19–24 we not only see Lamech's lineage, but also the development of culture (those who dwell in tents and have cattle, v. 20; those who play instruments, v. 21, and those who work with bronze and iron, v. 22). We also must note that there is not just a goodness recorded here for human culture imposes, at least to a certain extent, human will and desire over the other creational beings. There is also a negative quality noted here as well. It is Cain who went away from *Elohim* (to build the first city) and this negative quality is followed through in Cain's lineage, and specifically in Lamech to whom a direct comparison to Cain is made (v. 24).

Verse 25 turns back to Adam who knows his wife again, and she bore another son she called Seth (this genealogy is from the Yahwist authors). Now she again celebrates Seth's birth by saying, "*Elohim* has appointed another child instead of Abel, for Cain slew him (*Elohim* appointed rather than Eve purchasing, as in 4:1. And Seth's lineage starts with Adam)." In Eve's mind Seth just isn't another son (just a replacement for Abel and brother to Cain); but a son to replace Cain, the murderer. This starts another genealogy, the genealogy through Seth that, in Eve's mind, replaces Cain's. The two genealogy's names are too similar to just think that there are two separate cultures (perhaps there is, but we shouldn't just think that there is). Perhaps Seth's genealogy also observes that there is also a goodness in cultural development as a result of Seth's good genealogy. Verse 26 tells us about Seth's son Enosh. That it is in Enosh's time that humans began to call on the name of *Elohim* (another sign that Seth's genealogy is a replacement of, and certainly an alternative to, Cain's. But note that this calling on *Elohim*'s name is done by a pre-Israelite), and v. 26b emphasizes that, "At that time humans began to call upon *Elohim* (who were all pri-Israelites)." At least here there is now one/ones open to dialogue with some Other (this sets up the difference between Seth's genealogy and Cain's). The rest of the Seth's genealogy will be saved for the next chapter.

I must also restate my suggestion that *YHWH* from Gen 2 on must be informed by *Elohim* in chapter 1. Hence my emphasis of *Elohim*.

GEN 5

The chapter begins by addressing Seth's genealogy starting with Adam (these generations also start with the human male like the first narrative and are from the Priestly authors). This notes a new beginning for *Elohim* who also appoints Seth (similar to *Elohim* creating *adamah*), Eve doesn't purchase him like Cain; and yet it is not an entirely new beginning (and this new beginning is echoed in the flood in chapters 6–9). This new beginning refers to *Elohim* creating humans in the likeness of *Elohim* in v. 1 (this particularly recalls Gen 1:27 since 5:2 goes on to note, male and female). Verse 2 further states that *Elohim* blessed them with the name "man" [*sic*] (this value/opinion of the narrator should not be lightly dismissed, but our modern concepts calls this into question. It nonetheless affirms the same dignity before *Elohim* to the female as to the male. This verse provides the reason why from now on the human male along with the human female will usually be referred to as human, but the verse seems somewhat anachronistic if it simply is to inform chapters 1–4). Then v. 3 doesn't start with the birth of Cain (for, as I understand, 4:25–26 notes that he was replaced with Seth) and does start with Adam, and records Seth's heirs through v. 20. What is most notable is the length of life. But those numbers are vastly shorter when compared to other creation myths of the ancient eastern Mediterranean. Verse 21 elaborates on Enoch's life (and the rest of the genealogy is not a simple genealogy like what's listed in vv. 4b-20. The genealogy from Enoch on [21–24] becomes, in places, more descriptive); and v. 24 says, "Enoch walked with *Elohim*, and he was not; for *Elohim* took him."

Then v. 25 proceeds again with Enoch's son Methu'selah. Methu'selah becomes the father of Lamech and notes his length of life. Lamech is the father of Noah, and v. 29 specifically seems to record a prophecy about Noah, saying, "Out of the ground which Elohim has cursed (I question this cursing for I do not see *Elohim* cursing, only pronouncing the curse that a violation of the created order brings) and says this one shall bring us relief from our work and the toil of our hands." Verses 30–32 go on to note Noah's life and his sons' births: Shem, Ham, and Japheth.

One can see a similarity between the names of Seth's lineage in chapter 5, and Cain's lineage in 4:17–24. I think that this represents that, even though there perhaps were two distinct lineages, there was also a sharing of knowledge (cultural developments) between the two cultures. Can one really think that if there were only two cultures in the same vicinity that there would be no crossing or sharing of cultural knowledge? The cultural developments noted in Cain's lineage can be seen as both good (adopted by Seth's good lineage) and bad (developed under Cain's bad lineage). Each cultural development has both good and bad qualities (there seems to be a fluctuating ratio between the poles of good and bad that seems to be effected by time and circumstances).

I must also restate my suggestion that *YHWH* from Gen 2 on must be informed by the *Elohim* tradition in Gen 1. Hence my use of *Elohim*.

Chapter 5

THE FLOOD

Gen 6–9

GEN 6:1–5

Chapter 6 opens with a strange bridge into the story of Noah and the ark. It begins by noting that humans fulfilled part of *Elohim*'s command in 1:28 by "multiplying on the face of the ground," but one can question their fruitfulness. We've observed that fruitfulness does not simply imply multiplying (we have also noted that humanity's multiplication has resulted in the earth's destruction; both then and, as we see, now, given our current situation). Verse 2 records the strange relations between "the sons of *Elohim*, and the daughters of men [*sic*] who were fair; and they took to wife such of them as they chose." This seems to be a nod of recognition to other creation stories of the eastern Mediterranean region that Israel's parallels. They all have stories of heroic god-like characters. Verse 3 records the *Elohim*'s displeasure with the scenario, "My spirit/breath [the *ruach* of Gen 1:2, 2:7] will not abide in man [*sic*] forever, for they are flesh, but his days shall be a hundred and twenty years." Verse 4 notes that the Nephilim (the name is similar to the Hebrew word that means "fallen," and they reappear again in Num 13:33) are on the earth and says that these were the mighty men of old (as we noted above).

Verse 5 starts off the story about the flood by noting the pervasiveness of human wickedness (6:5 observes that the originating sin in chapter 3 has become a universal phenomena that affects all of creation (including the cosmic realm as well, and has truly become universal). The originating sin has now become the "original sin."

I must also restate my suggestion that *YHWH* from Gen 2 on must be informed by the *Elohim* tradition in Gen 1. Hence my use of *Elohim*.

GEN 6:5–22

Verse 5 starts off the story about Noah and the flood (the Yahwistic writer's beginning of the flood narrative) by noting the pervasiveness of human wickedness. *Elohim* saw that "Every imagination of the thoughts of man's [*sic*] heart was only evil continuously." Verse 6 accounts for *Elohim*'s sorrow in making humans. "It grieved [*Elohim*] to the [*Elohim*'s] heart [broken relationships affect *Elohim* like anyone else]." *Elohim* grieves (this echoes *Elohim*'s grief expressed in 3:22–23). And Fretheim also observes that this grief or pain is the same Hebrew word used to describe the human male's and the female's grief and pain in 3:16–17 (*Creation Untamed*, 59)! So in v. 7 *Elohim* says, "I will blot out man [*sic*] (this blotting out language establishes a purging theme that the rest of the scriptural canon develops) whom I have created from the face of the ground, man [*sic*] and beast and creeping things and birds of the air, for I am sorry that I have made them" (this verse specifically emphasizes humans, but all creation shares in the human's wickedness for it has affected even the cosmic realm as previously noted. Humans here, given the gift of domination for creation, are seen to represent all of creation, and have misrepresented dominion). This blotting out language in v. 7 seems to be final, but we encounter a further developing of the kenotic act of *Elohim* (which is further developed through chapter 11) because v. 8 continues by saying, "Noah found favor in the eyes of *Elohim*," thus supplying *Elohim* an alternative to total destruction (how humans live affects *Elohim* in either negative or positive ways).

Verse 9 begins P's flood story by introducing it (and the following narratives through chapter 8 are a weaving of the two stories from P and Y).

Verses 9–10 re-state Noah's righteousness (Noah walked with *Elohim*), and again records his sons Shem, Ham, and Japheth. Verse 11 restates the earth's evil in *Elohim*'s sight, referring to it as corruption (perhaps better said, creation has gone to ruin because of human activity [and inactivity by refusing to embody *Elohim*'s vocation/task given]), and as a result the earth was filled with violence. Verse 12 re-states that *Elohim* saw the corruption of all flesh, "All flesh had corrupted their way on the earth, or better said went their way as opposed to *Elohim*'s way [this is the controlling phrase throughout the flood narratives; 6:13, 17, 19; 7:15–16; 8:17; 9:11, 15–17]." It must be stated that the flood isn't some sort of punishment from outside of creation. It is an intrinsic result of human choices, the choices that occurred in chapters 3 and 4 (on the flood and the judgment of *Elohim* see Fretheim, *Creation Untamed*, 48–55). So in v. 13 *Elohim* tells Noah about being determined to make an end of all flesh, to destroy them along "with the earth." In vv. 14–16 *Elohim* tells Noah how to build the ark (though Noah's sons are mentioned twice, in 5:32 and 6:10, they are not recorded as helping Noah build the ark, nor is anyone else). Verse 16b notes that it is *Elohim* who shuts him in the Ark. *Elohim* tells Noah in v. 17 about destroying the earth with a flood of water so that all flesh that has the breath of life (*ruach*) will perish. Now, it must be noted here that it refers only to all flesh that has the breath of life. However, we have been arguing that it is just not all flesh that shares in the *Elohim*'s *ruach*; but that it is indeed all creation that shares in it, and in v. 13 *Elohim* talks about putting an end to the earth. And note that it is only after Noah has built the Ark that he learns the purpose for the Ark! In v. 18 *Elohim* tells Noah that *Elohim* will establish a covenant, and that it will be established with Noah, his sons, and his wife (this is the first talk of a covenant and is fulfilled in 9:8–17). Though none of the others in Noah's family are referred to as righteous (only Noah is) they are, nonetheless, included in the ark (perhaps as a concession to Noah's feelings? However, it is more probably due to *Elohim*'s impartial love). In v. 19 *Elohim* tells Noah that he is to bring two of every living flesh (both male and female), which *Elohim* brings to Noah, cf. 2:19, and continues this through v. 21. Verse 22 says that "Noah did this; he did all that *Elohim* commanded."

It is quite evident that this chapter (as well as 7 and 8) is a mixture of two strains of the story. One refers to *Elohim* and the other refers to *YHWH*. One story talks about evil, the other about corruption; one has doves, the other ravens; and one has general animals, the other both general and clean animals, but they both recount similar ideas.

I must also restate my suggestion that *YHWH* from Gen 2 on must be informed by the *Elohim* tradition in Gen 1. Hence my use of *Elohim*.

GEN 7

This chapter continues to weave the two separate stories concerning Noah and the ark. Verse 4 establishes a temporal limit to the flood. Verse 22 specifically notes that there is no distinction between the breath of life in animals and the breath of life in humans. All creation shares in *Elohim*'s breath of life (and we've been arguing that 1:2–3 notes that all creation received its being/life from *Elohim*'s *ruach*, not just humans or all flesh). The chapter follows the story through life on the ark and describes the flood before the waters recede in the next chapter. *Elohim* seems to forget Noah, the animals, and the ark, but the story is continued in chapter 8.

GEN 8

In 8:1 we find *Elohim* remembering Noah and all the beasts with him in the ark (this is reaffirmed In the first covenant, 9:8–17). And in v. 2 *Elohim* makes a wind, *ruach*. This is the second act by *Elohim* (6:17 and 8:2). The first action talked about concerned the disastrous affects in the flood story, but here looks forward to its salvation and the *ruach* blows over the earth (from whom all things came) causing the waters to subside (cf. Exod 14:21). In vv. 3–5 the waters recede from the earth continually, and the ark comes to rest upon the mountains of Ar'arat. In v. 6 Noah opens a window after forty more days, and in v. 7 sends forth a raven (the other story has doves) who flies to and fro over the waters until the waters were dried up from the earth (ravens and doves were commonly used by ancient mariners. And this raven flies to and fro until the waters are dried up, and he doesn't return to Noah; at least, we aren't told so). Then in vv. 8–9, the other story says Noah sends forth a dove to see if the waters have subsided from the earth, and that the dove returns, finding no place to land. Noah waits another seven days (seven being the divine number of completion because of the first seven days of creation) and again sends forth the dove, which comes back in the evening with an olive leaf in its mouth. Noah waits another seven days and sends the dove out again, and it doesn't return, so Noah leaves the ark. Verses 11–12 quietly address *Elohim*'s re-creation of plant life and the life of the earth. Verses 13–19 give the other story's account. In v. 15 *Elohim* tells Noah to go from the ark (in this account Noah doesn't decide on his own) along with his family and every living thing that is with him that they may breed abundantly and multiply on the earth (no talk of fruitfulness). Then, in v. 20, Noah builds an altar, and takes every clean animal and offers burnt offerings. In v. 21 *Elohim* is pleased with Noah's offering and comes to the opinion that "I will never again curse the ground because of man [*sic*] for the imagination of his heart is evil from his youth [*Elohim* recognizes this evil—this is another kenotic act. *Elohim* has chosen to be for humans and creation in spite of human evil. We have questioned whether *Elohim* curses anything, but v. 22 records that *Elohim* cursed the ground, which we question; though this comes from the Yahwist authors, we see some influence by the Priestly authors in that Noah offers clean animals in v. 20 which the J authors didn't know, but the P authors did. Hence "curse" would apply to both authors, but we see that it doesn't apply to

Elohim, at least not according to the usual thinking]; neither will I ever again destroy every living creature as I have done." It must be noticed that all creation came out of the waters in 1:2–3. So in order for *Elohim* to destroy the earth, or creation, what other way should *Elohim* destroy any part of creation other than with a flood, for all was created through water, 1:2–3? A flood is the only way *Elohim* destroys or needs to destroy. It is through water that *Elohim* creates and destroys. This also speaks of a divine self-limitation and furthers the kenotic act of *Elohim*. This limitation is another aspect of *Elohim*'s image. Perhaps we should also image it! *Elohim* recognizes the universality of the curse (the flood didn't end up ridding the world of sin, and certainly not humans. Sin affects even the righteous Noah, cf. 9:22. *Elohim* recognizes that "the imagination of the human's heart is still evil from the human's youth"), and that humans are unable to do anything about the curse—nor any other part of creation either (Elohim will have to do something, but *Elohim* will not curse, and allows for creation's continual creation).

If we tap into *Elohim*'s thought in vv. 21–22, *Elohim* seems to be thinking something like, "I have promised never to again destroy all things for the imagination of the human heart which still remains evil from human's youth. So now what do I do? For I have also promised to keep the earth alive through seedtime and harvest, cold and heat, summer and winter, day and night shall not cease." *Elohim* will make sure that this order, these functions, will continue as the established order that *Elohim* created. We are not at the close of the flood story.

I see the flood story through *Elohim*'s eyes and so must re-state my suggestion that *YHWH* from Gen 2 on must be informed by the *Elohim* tradition in Gen 1. Hence my use of *Elohim*.

GEN 9

Chapter 9 provides a break from the happenings of the first eight chapters but does not dismiss them in any way. In the three following chapters the text begins to move from the strictly pre-historical happenings recorded in chapters 1–8, by moving towards the patriarchal history recorded in 12–50, but we are still in pre-historical times.

The passage opens with *Elohim* blessing Noah and his sons with the original blessing (1:28a): "Be fruitful and multiply, and fill the earth (but there is a question concerning fruitfulness, and there is no mention of it or subduing, and in chapter 11 we see that they are not filling the earth). *Elohim* seems to allow for the human lack of fruitfulness and has chosen to suffer the moral evil of sinful human choices (8:22–23, is a kenotic event)." In v. 2 *Elohim* adds something not told before (but explains the world as we know it), "The fear of you and the dread of you shall be upon every beast of the earth and upon every bird of the air, upon everything that creeps on the ground and all the fish of the sea; into your hand they are delivered (there is good reason for this dread because humans chose not to embody *Elohim*'s dominion, but to reinterpret dominion terms of their own understanding concerning what dominion is to creations' detriment. It also allows for a human arrogance, and is a self-limiting concession by *Elohim*, but is not what *Elohim* desires. It does, however, allow for human freedom even though it goes against *Elohim*'s choice). Now, "every moving thing shall be food for you; and as I gave the green plants, I give you everything"; this is a divine self-limiting action by *Elohim* (and is perhaps a grace to relieve the toil of being vegetarian in the presence of thorns and thistles and in a world that is toilsome. Though the earth is still productive even in spite of our best attempts otherwise)." Verses 2–3 contrast Gen 1:28b–30 by contrasting its harmonious relationship in creation with a human tyrannizing relationship over creation (not *Elohim*'s dominion, but human dominion. However, *Elohim* will allow it). There is no mention of clean or unclean food, but in vv. 4–5 *Elohim* gives the following prohibition: "only you shall not eat flesh with its life, that is its blood [though meat is added as a food source the indiscriminate killing of animals is prohibited], for all will be judged." To separate *Elohim* the judge from *Elohim* of creation is dangerously inappropriate. And in v. 5 *Elohim* continues in requiring a reckoning of one's own lifeblood.

Here specifically from both humans (who continue to be highly valued), and also from the animals (who are highly valued as well). And then the passage continues by noting that the shedding of human blood will require the shedding of human blood (specifically mentioning brother. Not only noting that all humans are brothers, but specifically countering Cain's response to his brother), for humans were created (the word *bara'* once again appears in the creation of humans) in the image of *Elohim* (humans still have their dignity before *Elohim*, and this sanctification of human life is a necessity because of the moral code to which creation has been subjected. But also, at the same time, seems too anthropocentric in light of the web of relationships developed in chapter 1). The paragraph ends as it opened, with the original blessing.

Verse 8 opens the passage that talks about the first covenant (it ends in v. 17). It's interesting that the covenant is established (*quam*) here and not at the end of chapters 3, chapter 4, or 6:4. We find that the covenant isn't simply made with Noah and his descendants. Since it is the first, the covenant must first be established by *Elohim* as a way that *Elohim* will answer to the ruining of creation. This establishing of the first covenant by *Elohim* is unilateral and does not require any action of anyone other than *Elohim*. This is also the establishment of an atonement theme as the way *Elohim* will deal with sin in order to reconcile creation, and it is to inform all other atonement acts that follow, including what was accomplished through Jesus. It also reaffirms the purgatorial theme that we've already seen; and it must be stated that the first covenant, and therefore all succeeding covenants, are based upon creation in both its being and its need for reconciliation (Fretheim, *God and the World*, xiii–xiv). Noah is the human representative that is required for the covenant (for the covenant needed to be established with a human representative since the human was given dominion over creation which *Elohim* still honors). The original vocation/task was given in 1:28, and we see here that *Elohim* re-establishes the original vocation/task by establishing the first covenant with a human representative (the original blessing is reaffirmed in both vv. 1 and 7), and *Elohim* owns this covenant in v. 9. Since *Elohim* owns it can we do any less? We are still partners with *Elohim* and still have our dignity before *Elohim*. The covenant isn't simply established with Noah and his descendants, but with every creature (animate and inanimate). The text says, "every living creature," but with further thought we see that there is no limitation to what is commonly thought to be living (though it must be noted that this culture, the Judaistic culture [and it seems the later Christian cultures] do not consider vegetation, or other inanimate beings, as living). In chapter 1 we noted *Elohim*'s intimate presence to and relationship with all creation, and that all creation was therefore in intimate relation with, and present before, *Elohim*; and lives because *Elohim* lives. We also saw that every part of creation is in relationship with every other part of creation, for *Elohim* created from that which was already created, and with creation's help (all comes from and shares in *Elohim*'s *ruach* in 1:2–3). And so there is a web of relationships in creation as Fretheim observes (*God and the World in the Old Testament*), and that web is also a web of life (for all share in *Elohim*'s *ruach*).

In *God and the World* (10–13) Fretheim discusses the relationship between creation, redemption, and salvation. He observes that redemption comes out of, and is built upon, creation; and that salvation is similarly related to redemption. Creation and redemption are like two sides of the same door. They each have their own particulars, but intimately work together (just as one must have a door before there are two sides to the door, so there is creation before that creation needs redemption or salvation, and the two sides work together); and doors are used to get from one place to another (this also applies for redemption and salvation).

We also noted above that the covenant is unilateral. There is no part of creation that needs do anything (as though any part of creation could do anything) to uphold the covenant. This is also supportive of the difference between establishing and making that we noted above (only *Elohim* establishes, and separates, while both *Elohim* and humans can make—another part of *Elohim* that humans are to image). *Elohim* holds this covenant valid as long as there are rainbows in the sky (and as far as I know there are, and they represent the *Elohim*'s joy!). This furthers the kenotic act that we've been following since chapter 1 and has *Elohim* essentially saying to creation, "I don't care who you are, or what you've done—or haven't done. I will be in things in such a way as to reconcile all of my created relationships" (and we found out about those relationships in chapter 1).

Fretheim also observed a strangeness in God's divorcing of Israel in Jer 2–3. He observes that the divorce codes in the Torah do not allow for any possibly of reconciliation after a divorce has taken place (that is to say that remarriage to the divorcee after she has been married to another cannot take place), but the text records that God allows for reconciliation with Israel after Israel had divorced God, and Israel had married itself to Baal. Then God is a Torah breaker like Jesus was. But then the legal code of the Torah (as with any legal code) does not take the importance of relationships into question. God loves Israel (*Jeremiah*, 73–75, 89–90). And *Elohim* loves creation.

This first covenant recognizes that creation was before the covenant and is the reason for the covenant; creation is more important than covenants! *Elohim* also binds the divine self to limited options concerning how the *Elohim* will use power in the future. Power will now be somewhat limited in light of human freedom and creation's life (on *Elohim*'s suffering see Fretheim, *The Suffering of God*). In any case, as Fretheim says (*God and the World*, 115), "One must speak of a symbiotic relationship of ethical order and cosmic order." We saw in 6:1–4, 7 that how one lives in this world does have its affect cosmically.

In 9:8–17 we have the first covenant recorded. This covenant must be compared with the Jerusalem Council in Acts 15:2–35 (John B. Polhill, *Acts*, 322–40. It seems that the first covenant in Gen 9 seemed to have a prior importance regarding covenants in the early church). Verses 10–12 specifically notes that this first covenant is made with all living creation (cf. 9:12, every living creature, *kol-nepesh chayyah*; though the covenant specifically includes "all flesh" here it is expanded to include "every living creature" which includes much more than all flesh or even all living vegetation, but all living creatures; all the earth!), and that it is established for all future generations. This also begins an eschatological, and apocalyptic, answer to sin in the scriptural canon (for both the Older Testament and the Newer Testament. I'm indebted to Fleming Rutledge (*Advent*) for this apocalyptic insight. Though she observes this only for the Newer Testament (that it should be interpreted apocalyptically) I see that it also applies to the Older Testament in my essay "The First Covenant, Gen 9:8–17; and Its Fulfillment, Rev 18:1—22:7." This apocalyptic thought should also apply to the Older Testament, and there is a realized eschatology here.

Verses 18–19 observes Noah's sons (Shem, Ham, and Japheth), and that Ham (the son the next passage questions) fathered Canaan; and that the world was re-populated from these sons.

Verses 20–28 is the passage that tells of Noah planting the first vineyard (a somewhat easier task than other agricultural work in the day as it doesn't require annual plowing) and becoming drunk from the wine produced (drunkenness was part of Canaanite worship and, like its sexual practice, had enticing affects on Israel. Here the seduction is shown to be problematic for even the elect—like Noah). Noah is seen naked by Ham (it must be understood that to be seen naked in that culture is similar to treason in our culture) and follows with his report to his brothers Shem and Japheth, and their appropriate covering of Noah. Noah then curses Ham. This curse seems to be influenced by Israel's later history for it seems a rather unjust response by Noah, but it's part of the story (and helps to establish the world that Israel knew). The passage concludes with the account of Noah's death and his age, though vv. 27–28 seem somewhat unjust to Canaan.

Some think the passage is a combination of two stories (like chapters 6–8). One having Shem, Ham, and Japheth as Noah's sons, and the other having Shem, Japheth, and Canaan as Noah's sons. But this is only conjectural (Fretheim, *Creation, Fall, and Flood*, 117–21).

However, *Elohim* can be seen to say to Ham, "Ham, what you've done changes things, for it has serious implications for you, but in spite of that I will be with you and for you, as my covenant says. I choose not to revoke my covenant, or amend it in any way."

CHAPTER 6

GEN 1–9

Summary

It's noticeable given the placement of the start of Noah's flood (that it falls in the center of chapters 1–11, and I don't think this placement is haphazard), and given its length (three out of eleven chapters, much longer than any other story) that Noah's story is central to the understanding and interpretation of the theology of the first eleven chapters. I think the importance of the story is summarized in 9:8–17, the explanation and description of the first covenant.

Christendom, however, places the importance in Gen 3, which seems incorrect to me, and spins the understanding of the theology of Gen 1–11 (and the rest of the scriptural canon) in unfortunate and damaging ways. The rest of the Older Testament does not make reference to the events recorded in chapter 3, but it does refer to Noah's flood several times. So which story is to have informational influence over the rest of the scriptural canon? As Fretheim observes (*God and the World*, 262),

> Salvation language is used for the animal world as well for humankind, from the story of the flood (Gen 6:19; 9:10) to everyday activity ("you save humans and animals alike, O Lord," Ps 36:6) to the new heavens and earth (Isa 11:6–9; 65:25). God is as concerned with the

liberation of animals as with human beings [indeed with all creation]. Moreover, God rejoices and delights in God's relationship with the nonhuman order of things (see Ps 104:31; Job 38–39; see Prov. 8:30–331 on rejoicing).

And to quote Fretheim again, but this time out of *Creation Untamed*, 47:

> A basic list of what God does in the Genesis Flood story is remarkable: God expresses sorrow and regret; God judges but does not want to judge; God goes beyond justice and decides to save some, including animals; God commits to the future of a less-than-perfect world; God is open to change and is receptive to doing things in new ways in view of divine experience with the world; and God promises never to do this again. Even more, the story witnesses to a God who acts in judging and saving ways beyond the walls of the chosen community. Indeed, in the larger creational context in which the flood story is imbedded, God engages in a remarkable string of activities that the chosen community has often reserved for itself. God elects, reveals, saves from danger and death, and makes promises. And this long before Abraham! And the biblical story suggests long since Abraham. From the perspective of many a Bible reader, these are problematic images for God—and commentators often move past them too quickly. Some of these convictions that I detail make us all little uncomfortable theologically, or perhaps very uncomfortable. But I would like to invite readers to consider them and to think about how your theological perspective might be shaped by them.

Chapter 7

THE FIRST COVENANT, GEN 9:8–17; AND ITS FULFILLMENT, REV 18:1—22:7

Above we saw that the first covenant was established with all creation, and that it is a unilateral covenant established by *Elohim*. In essence *Elohim* says to all creation, "I don't care who you are, or what you've done; or haven't done. I will be in things in such a way as to reconcile all of my created relationships" (we've noted from chapter 1 this extensive relational web; and we noted that the first covenant, as all covenants, is based upon creation and its need for reconciliation, cf. Isa 54:9–10). And *Elohim* holds the God-self accountable to uphold this covenant. The covenant will be good as long as there are rainbows in the sky, and it is *Elohim* who (in partnership with creation) makes rainbows.

Now let's hear about the courtroom scene in Rev 20. Actually, there are two courtroom scenes in Rev 20. The first recorded, in 20:4b–6, is for the saints (all believers; not simply confessors, but those who embody the way of Jesus; which is ultimately up to *Elohim*'s discernment). And the angel says that they have no need to worry concerning the second death for it has no authority over those of the first resurrection (in verses 20:5–6 the first resurrection is discussed). However, the talk of a first resurrection makes a second resurrection possible (necessary). It is also noteworthy that while the first death has authority over those of the first resurrection the first death does not conquer the first resurrection (for the first resurrection overcomes the first death, and that the second death has no authority over those of the first resurrection). Not that the first death has no power over those of the first resurrection, for they too are subject to the first death (and they too are judged, but their judgment is to start in this world, cf. 1 Pet 4:17). However, judgment of condemnation has no authority over them for resurrection overcomes death and its judgment of condemnation (the judgment of *Elohim*'s affirmation overcomes the judgment of condemnation). But before we look at the second courtroom scene, perhaps we should set the stage for the second courtroom scene.

Revelation 19 is supposedly the "Armageddon" chapter, but Armageddon receives no mention here. It is mentioned only in 16:16 where it is the gathering place of all the evil spirits and *the nations and the kings of the nations* (Revelation's shorthand term for the disobedient this side of the first death). The scene in Rev 19:11–16 opens with the vision of a white horse with its rider who is faithful and true, and judges in righteousness (the rider is another image of the lamb/Jesus). His eyes are like a flame of fire (this echoes 1:14), and he wears many *diadems*, the golden circlet of kings, instead of the *stephanos* which he and his followers have been wearing up till now, for chapter 19 pictures the ultimate overcoming. The *stephanos* was the crown of grapevine wreath given in athletic victory. The evil spirits and the nations and kings of the nations wear the *diadema* (the golden crown representing a king's oppressive domination). This is an important image that Christendom's usual English translations don't recognize (consistently translating both, incorrectly, as crown) and therefore don't allow it to inform one's understanding of Revelation (this is not the only image that Christendom does not allow to inform one's understanding of Revelation).

Another image is the wordplay that appears in Revelation's use of the Greek word *nikao*. The play is between its definitions "conquer" and "overcome." The usual translations of Christendom (especially in English) offer no distinction between its definitions, but consistently translate it as "conquer." This seems to me erroneous. I suggest it should be translated according to what it qualifies, and only translated as "conquer" when it qualifies the oppressive dominating ways by which kings and the nations conquer (cf. 1 Sam 8). It should be translated as overcome when it qualifies Jesus' way, and the ways his followers overcome (cf. Rev 12:11). There are only two (possibly three) times in Revelation that it should be translated as "conquer." They also make the same mistake in Rom 12:21, but this time they consistently translate *nikao* incorrectly as "overcome." I suggest the proper translation should be, "Do not be conquered by evil, but overcome evil with good."

Revelation 19:13 sees the rider on the white horse wearing a robe dipped in blood and he is known as the word of *Elohim* (this image is of Jesus but notice the word *Elohim* speaks into the void in Gen 1:2–3). It is a picture of not only the white rider's blood, but ours also mixed in as well (cf. Rev 12:11). Jesus did not simply shed his blood for us, but also will judge us, requiring our blood (cf. Gen 9:5 and Rev 12:11). In v. 14 the armies of heaven are arrayed in fine linen (these are the saints for they are also white and pure cf. 6:9–11) who follow the white rider on the white horse also on white horses. Verse 15 tells us that a sharp sword issues from the white riders' mouth (who opens the passage) with which he will smite the nations (since words and tongues come out of mouths more often than swords I understand this to be a good picture of being convicted/slain by *Elohim*'s word. This can refer to both *Elohim* and/or Jesus). *Elohim*/he will rule them with a rod of iron (this echoes 12:5 which echoes Ps 2:9, and pictures *Elohim*'s strong rule that breaks opposition); and he will tread the winepress of the fury of the wrath of *Elohim* the Almighty (Almighty echoes Rev 1:8, and Revelation is the only book in the Newer Testament that refers to *Elohim* as the Almighty). He treads *Elohim*'s wrath for *Elohim* will judge all. Judgment, however, does not only consist of condemnation, it also consists of affirmation! Verse 16 says that on his robe and thigh is inscribed his name, king of kings and lord of lords.

Verse 17 begins a new paragraph, though it is the same vision, just another aspect of it. An angel calls out to all birds that fly in mid-heaven (sky) to gather for the great supper of *Elohim*; to eat the flesh of kings, to eat the flesh of captains, to eat the flesh of mighty men, and to eat the flesh of horses and their riders ("flesh," *sarx*, is repeated four times for emphasis, and four is the universal number; and is not simply the physical flesh. When Paul refers to the *sarx* he doesn't simply refer to the physical flesh). In v. 19 John sees the beast and the kings of the earth with their armies marching to make war against the rider and his armies on white horses (note that the beasts' armies march away from the place where they were gathered to make war. They were gathered in 16:16, where the word "Armageddon" actually appears, and so the place where they were gathered is Armageddon, not necessarily the place to which they march to make war in v. 19 (cf. 20:9)! But then there isn't any war. For v. 20 tells us that the beast and the false prophet (who was in the beasts' presence working false signs of deceit; in modernity this is known as propaganda) were simply captured without any mention of a battle and thrown into the lake of fire burning with brimstones. And then the next verse tells us the rest of the beast's followers were slain by the sword of him who sits on the horse, with the emphasis that this sword is the one that issues from his mouth (it presents a different conviction than the beast's and the false prophet who were simply captured! Though they too are thrown into the lake of fire); and the birds gorged on the flesh. Now back to the courtroom scene in 20:11–15.

The second courtroom scene is for the nations and the kings of the nations (Revelation's shorthand reference to the disobedient this side of the first death). The one seated on the throne (the Most High God's throne with Jesus seated on it, cf. Rev 4 and 5) has the dead come before *Elohim*/him (only the disobedient in Revelation are referred to as dead, not the saints), and books are brought out. I agree with Jacques Ellul (*Apocalypse*) that these books record all of human culture and history. It is these books that condemn them (but they have already spent some time in the lake of fire, cf. 19:20, now perhaps more is to come?). However, 21:8 seems to tell of their final lot, but is it their final lot? All the disobedient will be thrown into the lake of fire, which is the second death. But here it is not mentioned that the lake continues (so does it? And further in 21:24–27 we find the nations and the kings of the nations in the New Jerusalem) but 20:10 simply reaffirms their lot is the lake of fire. But in verse 21:4 we are told that death is one of the things that is no more (does this also include the lake of fire, the second death as well as the first death?). If they are punished again this would be a double jeopardy. However, another book is brought out which is the book of life (20:12c). It seems to trump their condemnation acquitting them, or does it? We read in 20:13a that the sea gave up its dead, as did death and Hades (the second death). When the Greek repeats a word or concept it acts to intensify it. In English we do the same thing, "it's not love, its love love." But here, in Revelation it's the death of death. This is not only the annihilation of the first death, but now this is also the death/annihilation of Death *and* Hades which now includes the first death and the second death, but only after Death and Hades has released their dead in 20:13c, and in v. 14 we find that Death and Hades themselves were thrown into the lake of fire!). Verse 12 implied that all the dead were judged by what they had done (the released dead and seems to begin a second resurrection which is pictured in 21:24–26). Do the disobedient get another turn in the lake of fire? No, for then that would say that double jeopardy is part of *Elohim*'s justice, and that the lake of fire still exists (it doesn't in 21:4, and in 21:24 we find the nations walking by the light in the New Jerusalem). So they were saved. Verse 20:15 says that "if anyone's name is not written in the book of life he was thrown into the lake of fire (but this is a judgment of an affirmation of salvation than anything cursed as belonging in the lake of fire which would be a double jeopardy for we are told in 20:14 that this is the second death, and with the death of death, the lake is no more), and it is the book of life itself that testifies for them (20:12).

By now one must wonder who or what of *Elohim*'s creation (which concerns much more than the human realm) is not listed in the book of life (cf. Gal. 3:21 where Paul links the law/Torah with life stating that the law is not against the promises of God (*Elohim*), or life. I'm indebted to Daniel Stramara Jr. for this insight (see his *God's Timetable*, 61). Chapter 20 redefines the usual thought regarding the book of life. It was the case that the book of life in the ancient world kind of played the role of a census. If one is in the book then one was a good citizen and so had all the opportunities, privileges, and responsibilities of any citizen (however, citizens were only males, and usually only the wealthier males at that). It was the case that if one didn't behave as a good citizen one could have their name removed from the book of life, and no longer have access to the rights, privileges, and responsibilities of a citizen. But can one think that *Elohim's hesed* (mercy, steadfast love, cf. Micah 6:8) is so limited as to throw one or another of *Elohim's* creation out of the book of life? That, for me, is to think that *Elohim* is so inept that *Elohim* can't redeem creation, and that *Elohim* doesn't really love the creation either; certainly not the wicked ones (contra Gen 9:8–17). But this scene disagrees with that assessment by picturing *Elohim's* mercy. *Elohim's* steadfast love (*hesed*) seems to control what we humans experience as *Elohim's* vengeance/wrath (*hesed* informs wrath enabling grief which is the divine side of *Elohim's* judgment of condemnation. The human side experiences judgment simply as wrath). However, *Elohim's* vengeance/wrath gets embodied differently than human vengeance/wrath/condemnation (*Elohim* is not human, certainly not a man). *Elohim's* vengeance/wrath/condemnation is controlled by *Elohim's hesed*. *Elohim's* wrath certainly gets played out but doesn't overcome *Elohim's hesed* (cf. Ps. 107:1, James 2:13). This second courtroom scene observes that and is pictured in 20:24. This is *Elohim's hesed* that triumphs over the judgment of condemnation.

In the first salvation scene (chapter 21) there is no temple in the city of the New Jerusalem for the whole city is a temple (the foursquare recording of twelve thousand stadia of 21:16 comprises the then-known world, and so we must think in terms of the whole world). This city, the New Jerusalem, encompasses both the bad cultural developments under Cain's heirs (which have now been cleansed of their evil, allowing for their original glory to be rediscovered, cf. 2 Pet 3:10 where the Greek text speaks of "will be discovered," *eurethasetai* which is usually not translated and is the last word in the Greek sentence. This word implies more of a reclaiming, and yet there is a re-birth, than one simply of reclamation) along with the good cultural developments under Seth's heirs (and notice that in 21:2 the New Jerusalem comes down out of heaven to earth thus once again uniting the celestial realm of *Elohim* and this cosmos. It's not that we get taken up to heaven. The holy city of the New Jerusalem comes down to us out of heaven). In v. 23 we find out that the city has no need for light because the glory of *Elohim* is its light that shines through the Lamb, and in v. 24 we find the nations walking in this light—wait, the disobedient nations we saw condemned in the last chapter are in the New Jerusalem? Not only are they in the New Jerusalem, but it continues by saying that the nations and the kings of the nations (the wealthy) bring their glory with them (some versions say wealth, and that is not wrong for the "glory" of a king and a nation is typically seen to rest in its wealth). Back in chapter 18 we have the common phrase that this, that, and the other thing "are no more." And most of the things (with the exception of slavery) are good things. So, at the end of chapter 18 one wonders why these good things are no more? Now we see them parading into the New Jerusalem along with the kings of the nations.

Psalm 82 has the Most High God judging the gods, or the heavenly council, and in v. 2 the Most High questions them: "How long will you judge unjustly and show partiality to the wicked?" The Most High, in verses 6–7, then speaks the judgment the Most High gives to them: "You are gods, sons of the Most High all of you, nevertheless, you shall die like men, and fall like any prince (even the wealthy and powerful). And Ps 82 ends, "Arise, O God, judge the earth; for to you belong all the nations" (RSV). For me that death is told in Rev 18:1—20:15 (the judgment of condemnation actuality occurs in 20:11–12b), but the final judgment of acquittal is told in 20:12c-15 and is pictured in Rev 20:12c—22:7. In 21:24 we find the nations, and the kings of the nations (the wealthy of the nations) bringing into the New Jerusalem their glory. This glory is judged in 18:1—20:15 (and concerns the judgment of condemnation that is overcome with the ultimate judgment of acquittal pictured in 20:12c—22:7), and their glory accompanies the dead of the nations. They died and were judged just like (the nations or humanity as the judgment in Ps. 82:6–7 records. But this glory later also enters the New Jerusalem along with the dead, and now alive nations; and kings of the nations. The gods that are mentioned in Ps 82 get no mention in the NT (Paul refers to them as the principalities and powers). They do, however, produce some good things, it's that their injustice overwhelms these good things; and it is *Elohim*'s judgment that they are no more (they were condemned to death like any mortal. Are they also raised like any mortal? Apparently, though Revelation doesn't explicitly say so. Instead it pictures the annihilation of Death and Hades 20:14), and the evil of the nations and the kings of the nations (cf. 20:11–12b), and not necessarily the annihilation of Satan (the devil, the dragon, the false prophet, or any of the panoply of evil. At least, by now, they've been so changed that their evil is no more for it has been annihilated). But, like any part of *Elohim*'s creation, they are saved (cf. 12c–15); for their wealth/glory comes in tow along with the nations and the kings of the nations, coming through the never shut gates of the New Jerusalem. Revelation 21:27 reaffirms (in case you wondered why they are here at all, especially with all their stuff), "that nothing unclean shall enter it (the New Jerusalem), nor anyone who practices abomination or falsehood, but only those written in the Lamb's book of life." All the glory of the nations, (their glory is ruined by sin, but 2 Pet 3:10 talks about their glory being found once again, *eurethasetai* (see this entire passage in 2 Pet 3:1–14). Their sin is now cleaned up, and they and their stuff are the true glory the *Elohim* intended. Revelation 21 is only the first vision of the final reconciliation, so we must follow the story through the second vision in 22:1–7.

Revelation 22 opens with the river of the water of life flowing from the throne of *Elohim* and the Lamb (this echoes Ezek 47). It flows through the middle of the city and has on either side the tree of life (and it must be noted that this is not just one tree, but is a forest of trees. This city also includes the forest which represents all of creation!) bearing its fruit throughout the year (with its twelve kinds of fruit at least one fruit seems to be produced every month. There's no more hunger, and note that this tree is a forest); and the leaves of the tree are for the healing of the nations. One must ask that if the nations are in the New Jerusalem why do they need healing? I suggest that the nations are in need of healing because anyone would after coming out of the lake of fire (not to mention anyone with disabilities of any sort; or anyone who has been or is subject to any disease or weakness of any kind). In v. 22:3, we are again reassured that even if these nations (the disobedient this side of the first death) are in the New Jerusalem (and specifically with all their stuff) "there will be no more anything accursed." In chapter 18 we hear of all kinds of good things that will be no more. Here in Rev 20:14—22:7 it refers only to something evil that is no more, for there will be no more anything accursed. But it is even more interesting and reassuring than that. For this Greek phrase *ouk estin eti* ("is no more") doesn't occur in chapter 18. But it does occur elsewhere in Revelation. The phrase also appears in 21:1, 4, 25, 27, and finally in 22:3, saying there will be no more sea (chaos), death, mourning, crying, pain, night (darkness), no more anything unclean, and finally no more anything accursed. These seven things make up the divine number seven and are the only things that are annihilated in Revelation. But then these things are the evil of chaos, and *Elohim* never did create chaos. Back in Gen 1:2–4 chaos is the disordered, unproductive, and nonfunctioning materiality that has no good purpose and just is; from out of which *Elohim* calls order; providing productivity, function, and good purpose. We have gone from the good garden in Eden to the perfect garden city the New Jerusalem; for the throne of *Elohim* and of the Lamb shall be in it, and *Elohim* and the lamb's servants shall worship *Elohim* and the lamb (these nations are now numbered among *Elohim*'s and the lamb's servants!). Verse 4 continues by saying, "they shall see *Elohim* and the lamb's face, and *Elohim* and the lamb's name shall be on their foreheads." We hear of night being no more, nor is there any need for light cause Elohim will be their light and they shall reign forever. In v. 6 we are assured that these words are trustworthy and true. And v. 7 assures us that God (I Am) is coming soon.

This is the greatest fairytale ending, but it is no fairytale! It is christological eschatology, and (it seems to me) is biblically sound. And it should be noted that we don't reach the fairytale ending without going through the pain, trials, and tribulations that lead into it. But it is the greatest fairytale ending!

"Amen. Come Jesus!"

I also need to say that I've come to read Revelation through *Elohim*'s eyes, but that it isn't significantly different from my understanding of Revelation at the start of this study.

GEN 10

The chapter provides the genealogies of Shem, Ham, and Japeth that 9:18 foresees and comes from the Priestly writers; and, as Birch observes, indicates that *Elohim* is in relationship with all nations (see his "Creation and the Moral Development of God in Genesis 1–11" in Gaiser and Throntveit, *"And God Saw That It Was Good"*, 22). This table of nations is from the priestly writers and understands that the division into races, cultures, and languages is the natural result of traveling peoples. Though it notices the divisions it insists on the essential unity of all humans.

The genealogies not only include their line of decent, but also tell us where those peoples lived (and the nations they became). They establish the eastern Mediterranean world that Israel knew. In v. 9 the character of Nimrod is introduced. He is a mystical character that certainly has a history behind his character. He is said to establish the nation of Babylon and some of its important cities.

The establishment of the nations from the genealogies seems to be out of place, for they occur before the scattering of the peoples in 11:8. But they're not really out of place as it establishes *Elohim*'s relationship with all nations.

GEN 11:1—12:4

The chapter begins by looking at the whole earth (the earth is the subject and the place of action) that had one language (tongue), and that being one with not many words. This story comes from the Yahwistic writers and notes that the divisions, both culturally and nationalistically, are a result of sin. Sin isn't just an individual phenomenon as noted in chapter 3. It affects all relationships. The breakdown of relationships, or sin, has developed from individual sin in chapter 3, to sin between brothers in 4:1–7, and between children and parents in 9:20–27; is developed as universal in this world 6:5–7; and affects the cosmos (all creation) as well as being universal (6:1–4), and now is also related to the life of nations. Though we have seen that humans have fulfilled part of the original blessing of 1:28 (they have multiplied), however, they have not fulfilled the aspect of filling the whole earth (nor have they necessarily been fruitful). Instead they are pictured as refusing to fulfill that part of the blessing (they are bunched together in their dubious fruitfulness). The Babel story may well be intended as a subtle (for political reasons, being under Solomon's rule) Yahwistic critique of the building of the temple under Solomon (which occurred during the time of the authors and is also an argument against the developing nationalistic YHWH cult). Fretheim goes on to say (*Creation, Fall, and Flood*, 126),

> [The authors] may have looked upon the temple as an attempt at the institutionalism of the place of meeting between man [*sic*] and God. Such an enterprise was dangerously close to the conception inherent in the ziggurats of Babylon—an enterprise to turn the God of heaven into a neighbor whose ways were fixed within the confines of an earthly building.

Verse 2 notes that humans migrated from the east (they migrated from the east because they went east out of the garden in 3:24) until they came upon the plain of Shinar and settled there (located east of Israel toward Babylon and became part of Babylon). A play on words occurs in the following verses between their wanting to be in one place (*sham*) and their desire to have "one name" (*shem*). In v. 3 they make bricks that are burned thoroughly and used bitumen mortar, both characteristic of Shinar/Babylon building (while there are many more rocks and stones in Israel, and this tower has its 'head in heaven' [sky]). Verse 4 notes that just building homes was not enough for them, but that they went on to build a city (cities at that time were centered around a temple mount, or ziggurat, that also served as the financial center; or the central gathering place of goods, power, and authority, as well as serving as the meeting place with the god). The end of the verse notes another reason for building a city ("let us make a name for ourselves"). In v. 5 *Elohim* goes down to check out what humans have been building (though the tower is high it is still in the sky, and *Elohim* must still go down to look at it). In v. 6 *Elohim* seems to recount what *Elohim* found before the council of the gods for the verse seems to be *Elohim*'s defense before the council of the gods, a defense for the following actions taken. *Elohim* (in v. 7) then asks the council to join *Elohim* in hindering what men [*sic*] have been doing by specifically confusing their language, because this building is only the beginning of the possibilities that the people can accomplish. Verse 8 records the result of that action as scattering (fulfilling a part of the blessing in 1:28 that was refused while being fruitful has already been acknowledged by *Elohim* as not simply possible for humans to fulfill, 8:21). But it must be noted that *Elohim* has chosen not to act alone, and that as a result, humans stop building (not just building in general, but specifically the building of the ziggurat city, the meeting place with god, and now it seems that because their language is confused the only other they can ask any advice from is *Elohim*). And v. 9 records that the area from which they were scattered is called *Ba'bel*, and gives the reason, "because *Elohim* confused their language (again focusing on the confusion of language, not simply the scattering). It must be noted that this passage says nothing about amending in any way, or abolishing, the first covenant. In essence *Elohim* says, "You nations?! This is still not a deal breaker with me. What you've done is serious and has its implications. But I choose not to abolish my covenant or amend it in any way. I will still be with you, and for you, whether you wish to be with me, or not." The story ends as it began by referencing "all the earth."

Verses 10–25 continues Shem's genealogy, and v. 26 introduces Terah (and his heirs that are developed in the following verses, vv. 27–29). Verse 30 specifically records that Sar'ai was barren. Verse 31 focuses on Abram who seemed to be the only one open to *Elohim*, and the following records his journey from Haran to Canaan (in *A Theological Introduction to The Old Testament* Birch, Brueggemann, Fretheim, and Peterson offer a good introduction and overview of Gen 1–11 [35–66]).

Revelation 12:1–4 is the important bridge between the prehistory described in chapters 1–11 to the history of the patriarchs of Israel. As Fretheim says, "The election of the family of Abraham and Sarah is an initially exclusive move for the sake of a maximally inclusive end" (*God and the World*, 19, 29). It begins by noting that *Elohim* said to Abram, "Go from your country and your kindred and your father's house to the land I will show you." In vv. 2–3 *Elohim* continues by blessing Abram (*Elohim* blesses Abram three times in the three verses!), "And I will make of you a great nation, and I will bless you and make your name great (this contrasts the human's attempt to get a name for themselves in 11:4b). Israel, through Abram, will be established and receive a name by *Elohim*'s doing so that you will be a blessing. I will bless those who bless you, and him who curses you I will curse; and by you all the families of the earth shall be blessed." Verse 3 ends by specifically noting that *all families of the earth* will be blessed through Abram. It must be noted that this passage says nothing about amending in any way, or abolishing, the first covenant, but re-establishes it (in a different way through Abram; but still it must be informed by the first covenant). Though the covenant is still universal, it now seems only universal among the nations; humans rather than the whole of creation (an anthropocentric turning but is only anthropocentric if it is not informed by the first covenant [9:8–17]). This seems to be an unjust and disturbing anthropological limitation if it is not informed by the first covenant (cf. Eph 1:9–10 and Col 1:15–20). And we've already seen Westermann's lament over this anthropological development of moving away too quickly from the creational theology developed in Gen 1–11). George Tinker rightfully understands that creation theology is better understood as a theology of community (*Spirit and Resistance*, 113). *Elohim*'s community. Verse 4 records Abram's journey from Haran to Canaan and leads into the patriarchal history of Israel.

CHAPTER 9

CONCLUSIONS

I argue that we see that the first features of *Elohim*'s character are first developed in Gen 1–11 (beginning to be revealed in Gen 1, but we should add chapters 2–3 as they are not meant to be separated from chapter 1) and are further developed throughout the following Scripture from Gen 4 onward. Both the OT and NT build upon that character developed in these opening chapters and is rightfully informed by, and is to be understood within, creation's, and *Elohim*'s, context, which we have discussed in our study of Gen 1–11. That character is of a social, relational *Elohim* of steadfast love who is the *Elohim* of all relationships, and therefore all societies (hence this does not allow for any hierarchialism, certainly not patriarchalism, for all parts of creation share the same value before *Elohim*, in other words their sacredness Tinker, *American Indian Liberation*, 38–44.). A part of the relationship of the relational *Elohim* is that *Elohim* shares the creative power with all of what *Elohim* creates and shares it in such a way that whatever affects one part of creation affects all other parts of creation, and *Elohim* as well (for all creation is in a web of relationships with each other and with *Elohim*, and *Elohim* with the entire creation. We noted that the earth was before creation began, and before the first day [1:4]. This is clear in the first narrative, as well as the second, and grounds creation in a place that is more spacially oriented than temporally oriented). We noted that this web of relationships in

Elohim's creation is preserved when the created relationships are served and protected by humans (*Elohim*'s dominion given in 1:26 and is further developed in 2:15). This dominion is *Elohim*'s gift to humans and creation and is one of partnership with the other (which is directly counter to the human understanding of dominion; that being the oppressive dominical quality over the other). If this creational relationship is not lived into by humans, then relational breakdown results—in other words, sin. Creation breaks down, and all creation (and *Elohim*) pay the consequences. We noted that sin does not come from *Elohim*, but comes from human choices, and the humans chose not to embody *Elohim*'s dominion, choosing their own idea what dominion is to be instead. Sin only enters into creation through human choice. As Birch et al. say, "Modern physics (quantum mechanics, chaos theory) has helped us see that this is not a closed system of cause and effect; there is a loose, if complex casual weave of 'play' within God's design that makes novelty, freshness, surprise, and serendipity possible (see Job 38–41)" (*A Theological Introduction to the Old Testament*, 271).

Verses 1:2–3 saw *Elohim*'s *ruach* (*Elohim*'s breath) hovering over the already-present deep void of darkness, and that the void of darkness was before *Elohim* began to create (however, not before *Elohim*). Apparently this void was not nothingness, there seemed to be some sort of materiality in it. However, we saw that this did not seem to contain anything that resembled a material that we know and experience. The material of the darkness was void of any order, productivity, function, and purpose, and had nothing what *Elohim* valued as good. We saw *Elohim*'s breath speaking (voice is an intimate presence that establishes relationship the other and informs that relationship) into this void of darkness creating light (we saw that the word "create," *bara'*, was never linked up with anything known as material and only has *Elohim* as its subject). We saw Elohim valuing the light as good (a good that has a purpose), and further separated the light from the darkness, giving it order, productivity, a good purpose, and instilling in it the function to realize that purpose (hence the ability to develop or evolve). This good purpose, and the function to realize that purpose, allows for a continuing creation (*Elohim* here shares the creative power with that which was created and valued as good to achieve its purpose, the light). *Elohim* called the light day and the darkness night, day 1. This light, its order and its productivity, good purpose and function had never been seen before. In the ensuing days we see that *Elohim* created from the light, which was created (thus establishing a web of relationships between *Elohim* and all creation, and between all created beings with each other, and *Elohim*).

Genesis 1:26–27 talks about humans created in the "image and likeness" of *Elohim* and is therefore a relational and social being because *Elohim* is. This image and likeness testifies to the overlapping spheres of power, roles, and responsibilities that *Elohim* shares with humans (but this special relationship is tempered with the noted reality that humans share day 6 of the first narrative with the creating of the animals). The larger aspect of this creational relationship goes way beyond the human realm to include all creatures, all creation. Through this "image and likeness" language the special relationship between *Elohim* and humans is established and described (though the relationship is still not anthropocentric). Humans are relational and social beings because *Elohim* is relational and social, and are to carry on a dialogical partnership with *Elohim* for creation (aspects of *Elohim*'s dominion. We noted other images of *Elohim* that humans are to image. They include [though probably are not limited to] relationality instead of independence, the ability to value (and that all creation shares in the same value), the sharing of power, the capacity to image *Elohim*'s understanding of dominion, and the humility of a self-limiting of kenosis). In 2:15 we saw how the two verbs *abad* and *shamar* ("to serve" and "to protect") show how the usual concept regarding stewardship for the land is vastly bankrupt. For the creational web also brings the rest of creation into an important relationship and partnership with both humans and *Elohim*. This relationship allows for all creation to share in *Elohim*'s creational power (this kenotic act by *Elohim* implies a mutuality in vocation among all creation. It also establishes a divine self-limitation for *Elohim* and that *Elohim* doesn't just dictatorially control how creation will develop but shares that development with creation).

Elohim is particularly concerned about the wrongful non-loving treatment by humans over any part of creation, and judges (and condemns) any treatment that is one of disrespectful non-love (for such activity is counter to *Elohim's* image). We also observed that Gen 2:5 notes that humans are as important to the creation as is water. We also saw *Elohim* breathing into the human life. This breath is *n'shamah* which makes the human *human*, and was later developed into the Hebrew *nephesh* (the self which links to the soul; and one's spirit with the Spirit). We saw that *Elohim* is panentheistic (*Elohim's* breath, the *ruach* of Gen 1:2, is within all things for all creation is developed out of, or through *Elohim's* *ruach* breath), and is also a Creator who is more henotheistic than simply monotheistic (however, monotheism is to be more informative of henotheism than polytheism).

The creation presented in Gen 1 and 2 is never presented as a done and finished product that is perfect. These chapters picture a continuing creation (that is particularly established by the establishing of the function of the good purpose of its creatures. Creation starts by recognizing a goodness, not evil or sin), which is very good for its purpose. We also noted a problem that usually results in sin and is the first evaluation by *Elohim* that something is "not good" in creation (in 2:18 it is not good that the human should be alone, or independent, for *Elohim* is not alone, or independent; and chooses not to act alone. This aloneness and independence does not image *Elohim*). *Elohim* proceeds (in the following creation of animals) to try to remedy this problem with the creation of animals and leaves the evaluation up to the human (this human ability to value creation also images *Elohim*). The human does not give a positive value to *Elohim's* work (in 2:20, the value is not sexual, but has more to do with companionship and partnership). *Elohim* tries again to remedy the problem (*Elohim* Yahweh can, and does, learn from the past), and again leaves the valuing up to the human. The creation of animals does not fulfill the human's need and so a second attempt to address the "not good" is needed.

Elohim cannot simply fill the need by *Elohim*'s presence alone. A new creation must hopefully fill the human's need, and must create something new. This time the value is extremely positive (2:23, the problem seems addressed; or is it?). This is also when the human becomes the human male (for we noted that with the creation of the woman there is now, for the first time in this story, a woman to lend the distinction that renders the human into the human male).

We observed that the language in 3:1–7 is descriptively interesting. The "you" in 3:1 is plural (therefore implying that the human male is present during the whole scene as the "we" in 3:2 suggests), and that in v. 4 the "you" is singular because the serpent is talking specifically to the woman (for it is she that answers in 3:2–3). But in 3:5 the serpent's language changes and the "you" and the "your" are once again plural because the serpent is now addressing both the woman and the human male (the "you" in vv. 1 and 5 should both be translated as "you all," and 3:6 implies that the human male is present). We also noted the disturbing rise again that something is not good. This "not good" mirrors the "not good" in 2:18, only this time it is specifically brought into connection with the choices that both the woman and the human male make, and they each refuse to discuss the question the serpent poses with each other, *Elohim*, or any other part of creation. They just come to their conclusions by themselves. This is an individualism that is every bit as singular as the human was in 2:18 (this presents an opposition between the community, in the web of relationships, and the individual human). We also noted the first grieving *Elohim* experienced is recorded in 3:22–23, or, better said, not recorded in the pause between 22 and 23. Some of the newer Hebrew scholars understand the pause to be the way early Hebrew expressed deep emotion. This grieving better fits the passage and is further echoed in 6:6; where *Elohim*'s grieving is recorded and is specifically accompanied with judgment (the judgment of condemnation, in human experience known as the *Elohim*'s wrath). Here, in 3:22–23, we sort of have *Elohim* saying, "What I really wanted was for the humans to serve and protect my garden and stay in my garden—but now . . ." And with that grieving the humans are expelled from the garden, but with no less dignity in *Elohim*'s eyes. This also furthers the kenotic theme in that it pictures *Elohim* who will embrace a development that produces suffering and grief in *Elohim* because the development is counter to *Elohim*'s desire. Yet *Elohim* chooses to suffer rather than to refuse to embrace the counter development.

Creation, because of sin, is not the fullness it was meant to be. *Elohim* is seen as judge in chapter 3 (but both a judge of condemnation, 3:11–24, and affirmation, 3:21), and records a judge who is seemingly wrathful in 3:14–19; but we also saw that wrath/wrathfulness is not simply a part of who *Elohim* is (wrath, in the negative, is a human experience, but that the *Elohim*-side of wrath is the positive reaction of grief). Wrath is only a result of human sin (if there was no sin then there would be no wrath, we bring it upon ourselves). And we also note that there is an order in creation that is affected by sin (which thus adds a human moral order). The order of creation can be experienced as floods, tornadoes, drought, and the flow of the seasons. These occurrences are naturally part of creation; but the following are similar and somewhat different. This moral order is enacted by sin resulting in holes in the ozone, deforestation and raging wildfires, and the current mass extinction of animals. All of which have a human cause (at least in their severity). In essence global warming, which is usually experienced as *Elohim*'s wrath (but is human caused, and grief is the *Elohim* side of wrath). This is readily noticeable in the earthly environment (and through the rest of the cosmos), but sin is particularly a human problem, and this violence is a result of human choices.

We also saw that the individual theme is further developed in 4:1–7. It is particularly evident in Cain's response to *Elohim*'s choice in 4;4, and in Cain's response to *Elohim*'s question in 4:7. 4:7 is also the first use of the Hebrew word for sin (*avera*). And we have also seen that sin, rather than something that just happens to us, is the result of human responsibility. It is the result of the human handing over one's control of the ego from the community (the web of relationships) to the individual self. The self decides for itself to live for itself rather than for the community of all creation, and we are told this is sin!

Cain denies *Elohim*'s questioning of him with the statement, "I didn't know I was to be my brother's keeper." This denial is the further development of the individual into the ego of the individual and dismisses *Elohim*'s question. Cain makes up his own mind without discussion with anyone (not *Elohim*, the human male, Eve, or any other part of creation). And that since the following development of culture in 4:17–24 is part of the same story it can be seen as both a good and an evil. However, culture must not be seen as simply good or evil. The good of Seth's following genealogy is seen as bringing a good aspect to culture. It must be understood as a mixture of both good and evil. Evil resulting from Cain's bad genealogy and the good leading to Seth's good genealogy.

Chapter 5 begins by recording Seth's genealogy (mentioned in 4:25) as the alternative to Cain's genealogy. It ends by noting Noah, leading into the flood account in 6:5—9:17, but first records in 6:1–4 that sin has gone beyond the universality of the earthly realm to encompass the cosmic realm; and 6:5 records that sin (originating in 3:1–7) has now become original in that it both unavoidably affects all of creation, and is also cosmic in its affect (humans are incapable of escaping sin). We noticed that the blotting out language in 6:7 establishes a purging theme that the rest of scriptural canon develops.

In human society (and the rest of creation) there will always be the disadvantaged needy. Humans were given dominion over creation (to image *Elohim*'s dominion). They therefore have an advantaged position over the rest of creation, and not just needy humans. All are to be cared for in the loving respectful way of *Elohim*. This dominion is given humanity by *Elohim* to serve and protect creation, cf. 2:15 (the original vocation/task given humans by *Elohim* for creation) and concerns not only needy humans, but also the other disadvantaged aspects of the rest of creation as well.

We noted that that the flood story is the central story both because of its position (in the middle of Gen 1–11) and because of its length (by far the longest story). And, in our estimation, is brought to its end with the establishment of the first covenant (9:8–17).

This first covenant is *Elohim*'s ultimate decision about atoning for sin. The first covenant in 9:8–17 is how *Elohim* chooses to reconcile creation; by addressing human sins, and our refusal to honor and own the establishment of *Elohim*'s dominion by maintaining creation through the serving of, and protecting of, the created relationships. And so this covenant must be established with human representation (for humans still have their original dignity before *Elohim*). Noah (representing humans and all of creation) has an advantaged place in the created order and is to care for the needy disadvantaged in all the cosmos. We noted that this first covenant is unilateral and that *Elohim* establishes this covenant with ALL creation (holding no part of creation responsible for the covenant. *Elohim* only holds the God-self responsible for the covenant). In essence *Elohim* says, "I don't care who you are, or what you've done or haven't done, I will be in things in such a way as to reconcile all of my created relationships (and we began to find out about those relationships in Gen 1)." This also establishes a self-limitation (a divine self limitation!): "never again shall all flesh be cut off." This first covenant is *Elohim*'s first (and defining) attempt to re-establish a proper relationship between humans and the rest of the cosmos (to restore all of creation). The ongoing vocation of *Elohim*'s followers (given to humanity in 1:26, the gift that is to embody *Elohim*'s dominion) continues to be claimed, but now starts with Noah (a pre-Israelite), leading to Abraham (also pre-Israelite) and then Israel, but which I understand is best embodied through Jesus. There are many reasons I think this, but above I see that the first covenant is most specifically fulfilled, and echoed, in the covenant made through Jesus (and represented most fully in Rev 18:1—22:7).

We noticed that 9:21 records a weird scene about Noah becoming drunk and Ham's wrong response, which continues the recording of familial problems (and is continued several times throughout the rest of Genesis), and the seemingly unfair punishment of Canaan. It does more than simply to continue familial problems (first seen in 3:16b). We noted that it also serves as a warning that even the righteous elect (Noah) are also affected by sin, and that drunkenness and sexual perversion were both part of Canaanite religion. It also leads into the story in chapter 10 where the genealogies of the nations are set up (all of which are affected by sin).

We noticed that the genealogies in chapter 10 seem somewhat out of place in coming before the scattering recorded in 11:7, but that they are not really out of place. We noted the bad desire "to make a name for ourselves" in 11:4 and we also noted that the story of Babel in chapter 11 perhaps serves as a warning against building the temple in Jerusalem as the authorship of story comes from the same time as the building of the temple (a subtle critique of building the temple as the authors were also subject to Solomon's kingship, and a critique against the developing nationalistic YHWH cult). It also pictures *Elohim* who does not act alone (either in creating or in judgment). For *Elohim*'s reporting 11:6–7 echoes the "Let us" in 1:26. We noted that the scattering answers *Elohim*'s command in 1:28 to fill the earth (not just to multiply which this story notes or be fruitful. Humans have too abundantly fulfilled multiplying given the over population problem, and their fruitfulness has never really been achieved, though they now are scattered over the earth).

This is my reading of Gen 1–11 and is a result of my suggestion that Gen 1–11 must be influenced by *Elohim* in chapter 1, and that the following must echo *Elohim*.

In their introduction to the OT theology Birch et al. makes the following comment in their discussion of wisdom literature:

> At times, there can hardly be any doubt that the *world willed by Yahweh* is equated with *the world in which we [humans] have advantage*, so that creation theology [the theology developed in Gen. 1–11 that we have been discussing] is confiscated and reshaped as self-serving ideology. No doubt this is a temptation for every socializing community. At the same time, however, we notice that creation theology acts as a check upon *ideological advantage* (*A Theological Introduction to the Old Testament*, 382, their italics).

BIBLIOGRAPHY: SOURCES CITED

Abram, David. *Becoming Animal: An Earthly Cosmology.* New York: Vintage, 2011.

———. *The Spell of the Sensuous: Perception and Language in a More-Than-Human World.* New York: Vintage, 1996.

Birch, Bruce C., et al., eds. *A Theological Introduction to the Old Testament.* Abingdon: Nashville, 1996.

Borgman, Paul. *Genesis: The Story We Haven't Heard.* Downers Grove, IL: InterVarsity, 2001.

Chesterton, G. K. *Collected Works of G. K. Chesterton.* San Francisco: Ignatius, 1986.

Collins, C. John. *Genesis 1–4: A Linguistic, Literary and Theological Commentary.* Phillipsburg, NJ: P&R Publishing, 2006.

Cullmann, Oscar. *Immorality of the Soul or Resurrection of the Dead? The Witness of the New Testament.* Eugene, OR: Wipf & Stock, 2010.

Davis, Ellen. *Getting Involved with God: Rediscovering the Old Testament.* Lanham, MD: Rowman & Littlefeild, 1970.

———. *Proverbs, Ecclesiastes, and the Song of Songs.* Westminster Bible Companion Commentary. Louisville: Westminster John Knox, 2000.

Deloria, Vine, Jr. *Evolution, Creationism, and Other Modern Myths.* Golden, CO: Fulcrum, 2002.

Eisler, Riane. *The Chalice and the Blade: Our History, Our Future.* San Francisco: Harper & Row, 1987.

Ellul, Jacques. *Apocalypse.* New York: Seabury, 1977.

———. *The Meaning of the City.* Lanham, MD: Eerdmans, 1970.

Fretheim, Terence E. *Creation, Fall, and Flood: Studies in Genesis 1–11.* Minneapolis, MN: Augsburg, 1969.

———. *Creation Untamed: The Bible, God, and Natural Disasters.* Baker Academic, 2010.

———. "Divine Dependence Upon the Human." *Ex Auditu* 13 (1997) 1–13.

———. *God and the World in the Old Testament: A Relational Theology of Creation.* Nashville, TN: Abingdon, 2005.

———. "The God of the Flood." *Calvin Theological Journal* 43 (2008) 21–34.

———. *Jeremiah*. Smyth & Helwys Bible Commentary. Macon, GA: Smyth & Helwys, 2002.

———. *The New Interpreter's Bible*. Vol. 1, *General and Old Testament Articles, the Books of Genesis, Exodus, and Leviticus*. Nashville, TN: Abingdon, 1994.

———. *The Pentateuch*. Interpreting Biblical Texts Series. Nashville, TN: Abingdon, 1996.

———. *The Suffering of God: An Old Testament Perspective*. Philadelphia: Fortress, 1996.

———. *What Kind of God? Collected Essays of Terence E. Fretheim*. Edited by Michael J. Chan and Brent A. Strawn. State College, PN: Eisenbrauns, 2015.

Gaiser, Frederick J., and Mark A. Throntveit, eds. *"And God Saw That It Was Good": Essays on Creation and God in Honor of Terence E. Fretheim*. St. Paul, MN: Word & Word, 2006.

Gowan, Donald. *From Eden to Babel: A Commentary on the Book of Genesis 1–11*. Grand Rapids: Eerdmans, 1988.

Kidwell, Clara Sue, et al., eds. *A Native American Theology*. Maryknoll, NY: Orbis, 2001.

Kimmerer, Robin Wall. *Braiding Sweetgrass: Indigenous Wisdom, Scientific Knowledge, and the Teachings of Plants*. New York: Penguin, 2018.

———. *Gathering Moss: A Natural and Cultural History of Mosses*. Corvallis, OR: Oregon State University Press, 2003.

Kissileff, Beth, ed. *Reading Genesis: Beginnings*. Bloomsbury: T. & T. Clark, 2016.

Kreider, Alan. *The Change of Conversion and the Origin of Christendom*. Eugene, OR: Wipf & Stock, 1999.

———. *The Patient Ferment of the Early Church*. Grand Rapids, MI: Baker Academic, 2016.

———. *The Origins of Christendom in the West*. London: T. & T. Clark, 2001.

LeFebvre, Michael. *The Liturgy Of Creation*. Downers Grove, IL: InterVarsity, 2019.

Lewis, C. S. *That Hideous Strength*. New York: Scribner's, 2003.

Morrow, Susan Brind. *Wolves & Honey: A Hidden History of the Natural World*. Boston: Houghton Mifflin, 2004.

Polhill, John B. *Acts: An Exegetical and Theological Exposition of Holy Scripture*. The New American Commentary 26. Nashville, TN: Broadman, 1992.

Primavesi, Anne. *From Apocalypse to Genesis*. London: Burns & Oates, 1991.

Quinn, Daniel. *Ishmael*. New York: Bantam/Turner, 1995.

Rutledge, Flemming. *Advent*. Grand Rapids, MI: Eerdmans, 2018.

Schroeder, Gerald L. *The Science of God: The Convergence of Scientific and Biblical Wisdom*. New York: Broadway, 1998.

Shroyer, Danielle. *Original Blessing: Putting Sin in Its Rightful Place*. Minneapolis, MN: Fortress, 2016.

Simard, Suzanne. *Finding the Mother Tree: Discovering the Wisdom of the Forest.* New York: Alfred B. Knopf, 2021.

Starks, Kenton. *"Fake News." Theology.* Eugene, OR: Cascade, 2020.

Stramara, Daniel F., Jr. *God's Timetable: the Book of Revelation and the Feast of Weeks.* Eugene, OR: Pickwick, 2011.

Tanakh. The Jewish Publication Society, 1985.

Tinker, George E. *American Indian Liberation: A Theology of Sovereignty.* Maryknoll, NY: Orbis, 2008.

———. *Spirit and Resistance: Political Theology and American Indian Liberation.* Minneapolis: Augsburg Fortress, 2004.

Trible, Phyllis. *God and the Rhetoric of Sexuality.* Minneapolis, MN: Fortress, 1978.

Walton, John H. *Genesis: The NIV Application Commentary.* Grand Rapids, MI: Zondervan, 2011.

———. *The Lost Worlds of Genesis One.* Downers Grove, IL: InterVarsity, 2009.

Westermann, Claus. *Creation.* Translated by John J. Scullion. Minneapolis: Fortress, 1974.

———. *Genesis 1–11: A Commentary.* Minneapolis, MN: Augsburg Fortress, 1974.

Wohlleben, Peter. *The Hidden Life of Trees: What They Feel, How They Communicate—Discoveries from a Secret World.* Random House, 2015.